LIFE

LIFEWORKS

AN INTEGRATIVE APPROACH TO HEALTH AND HAPPINESS

Dr. Aimee Harris-Newon

YouSpeakIt

PUBLISHING

*The Easy Way
to Get Your Book
Done Right™*

To you, the reader, for seeking more truth, health, and life—in every aspect of living. And to every brave being that came before me to bring a message of hope, inspiration, and knowledge to help pave the way for our current understanding of how to live life from the inside out—holistically, freely, and fully.

Contents

Acknowledgments

First and foremost, I want to thank Misty Kirkconnell, RPh, integrative pharmacist and health advocate extraordinaire, for the many ways she has opened my eyes to the myriad forms of healing outside of our traditional Western mindset and for her grit and determination in reclaiming her own health, all the while helping and inspiring countless others along her journey.

I'd also like to thank the entire team at YouSpeakIt Publishing for helping to make this project a reality, not just a dream or a goal. Special thanks to Amy for her patience, wisdom, and support.

Of course, I have to thank God and all of my invisible friends for this life of beauty and purpose that continues to unfold before me every single day.

I'd like to thank all my mentors—too many to list, but you know who you are—including the late Dr. Wayne Dyer, for the lifelong inspiration I've received from his teachings, along with Dr. Bernie Siegel, one of the most funny, compassionate, and wise physicians and healers I've had the pleasure to learn from along the way through his books and teachings.

I thank my extraordinary team of healers and coaches at Dr. Aimee and Associates and The Center for Integrative and Functional Health and Wellness for their continued high-caliber care and unwavering commitment to our vision of global health and wellness, and their commitment to our clients' and patients' highest and best interests. The comprehensive and innovative whole-person care they deliver is unmatched. Lasting change can't happen without the support of many, and they know, and live, the values we espouse of living life fully in body, mind, and spirit.

And last but certainly not least, I want to thank my wonderful life partner and wife, Renee, for the ways she inspires me, challenges me, and loves me completely; and to my moms, who have since passed on, for their lifelong belief in me and their constant support of my dreams and my goals, and my family who has always been there to love me and cheer me on.

Introduction

This book is about the general principles of healthy, abundant living. I must say that it does not boast of being comprehensive in its field. Neither is it intended in any way as a substitute for regular professional medical care, financial advice, or other professional guidance. Instead, this book is designed to introduce you to the myriad ways you can create a full, healthy, and satisfying life from a holistic perspective.

As you've probably heard before, "There are many roads to the top of the mountain."

This book is designed to be a user-friendly introduction to helpful information and simple strategies that are practical, easy to apply, and manageable enough to be sustainable over a lifetime.

I wrote this book because I genuinely believe and feel that the entire human race deserves a life of good health, satisfying wealth, and happiness. These states of being can be achieved despite anyone's past, or current, circumstances. Anyone can improve the quality of their life if they have a sincere and burning desire to do so. But desire alone is not enough for lasting change. One needs to know how to achieve the best outcomes, and that includes drawing on education, information, and instruction.

I hope you apply the information you learn from this book to develop and grow a sense of mastery and healthy control over all aspects of your life—body, mind, and spirit.

For best results, I recommend reading the book in its entirety to get a broad understanding of the general principles before applying the action steps or information. Then spend some time reviewing the areas of your life that you want to improve, such as your physical health. You may wish to lose weight or become more physically fit and active, or perhaps you need to change your perspective on your life. Perhaps you need to examine your relationships to determine if they really are supportive. Or maybe you need to review your financial mindset and habits.

Once you determine which aspects of your life are most essential for you to improve upon, you can define the specific action steps you need to take to achieve your goals in that area. Take change slowly, incrementally, and progressively for sustainable results.

I sincerely hope that you will gain true independence physically, financially, and emotionally as you learn better ways to approach your health.

What does it mean to live freely and independently?

It means to:

- Have good physical health
- Have ample energy and vitality to do the things you need and want to do
- Have the financial resources to live abundantly and invest in your own healthcare
- Design the life you want to live
- Live an emotionally balanced life
- Choose a life of peace, harmony, and happiness

If you want to be entertained, I am sure there are better reads than this book. If you wish to change your life or the lives of those around you, read on. Read on.

Chapter 1

THE WORLDWIDE HEALTHCARE CRISIS AND THE POLITICS OF HEALTH

Despite the seemingly impressive strides made in the field of medical science over the last sixty years, we, as a species, are not growing healthier. Therefore, achieving a higher level of health and wellness for the more significant percentage of the world's population is becoming harder by the day.[1]

Critical proof of this is seen in the failure to achieve the limited Millennium Development Goals in the areas of health in underdeveloped countries. You can also see it in the threat of infectious diseases caused by poverty, which is growing daily.[2] Add that to the increasing burden that chronic diseases impose on people's lifestyles. These challenges are further compounded by what is perhaps the most significant global economic crisis since the 1930s. They are likely to become much more severe in the coming years.

Social injustice, as well as unstable consumption patterns that waste and deplete already limited resources, contribute to the current economic crisis. There is a disconnect between rapid economic growth and advances in science, technology, and medical care, and the ability to manage these advances to better the lives of the global population.

Statistics from the World Bank show that the real-world annual income shot up from $25.096 trillion in the late 1990s to $71.845 trillion as of 2009.[3] Furthermore, modern-day advances in medicine and pharmaceuticals are majorly driven by market forces. The statistics are as staggering as they are alarming.[4] The discoveries in medical science have only benefited about 20 percent of the world's population.[5] Eighty-nine percent of the annual global health expenditure in 1990 was spent on only 16 percent of the world's population who somehow alone bear 7 percent of the burden of disease globally (when adjusted for disability life-years). The annual per capita expenditure ranges from about $6,000 in the United States, which forms about 17 percent of the GDP (Gross Domestic Product) to less than $10 in the least developed nations in Africa, which are about 3 percent of the GDP.[6]

These numbers paint a quite a grim picture. As advanced as we believe our medical science is, it has not translated into a healthier society for everyone. Relatively speaking, our level of healthcare is not much better than during the times we called *primitive*. The effects that politics and lobbying have on healthcare are worsening the situation even now. For example, researchers have noted that votes made in Congress have a significant impact on how trillions of dollars are spent in healthcare. This is the reason why the healthcare industry makes the most prominent lobbyists. It is quite a shame that a sector which is meant to be all about the patients and caring for them is now more of a lucrative industry.

Where are we getting it wrong? Why are the billions spent on research, development, and deployment of drugs and other medical and healthcare materials not yielding the results that we expect them to? Why are you spending so much for so little? But more importantly, what can you do about it? How can you avoid the adverse effects of this reality? If it turns out that the government and significant medical care firms are either unable or unwilling to provide the best level of healthcare and healthcare options, you must figure out what your own alternatives are and how you can best accomplish them.

THE EVOLUTION OF MEDICINE

People need to understand how medicine and modern healthcare have evolved from our earliest times. Since the beginning of time, the Earth has naturally provided everything we need to heal ourselves. It's quite remarkable in that regard.

The Creator executed a grand plan in which everything we need to be healthy is provided—flower essences, integrative and functional medicine, energy healing, healthy food, and clean water—and our bodies are created perfectly with an innate capacity for healing. The formation of a scab on a wound, although simple in appearance and function, is a beautiful example of the body's remarkable ability to heal itself.

If we are to improve the future of healthcare, we must get back to the basics by understanding where we've been, where we are now, and where we're going. With the knowledge of the evolution of medicine, we can determine the best solutions for those aspects of modern healthcare that don't serve us.

TRADITIONAL AND ALLOPATHIC MEDICINE

Allopathic medicine describes the kind of medicine that we are familiar with and is also called *conventional, Western,* or *traditional medicine.* Let's take a brief, but structured look into allopathic medicine, its history, and evolution.

The term *allopathic medicine* was coined in the early nineteenth century to differentiate between two types of medicine: *homeopathy* and allopathy. Homeopathy is based on the theory that "like cures like," and minute doses of the substances that cause a disease's symptoms could help cure the disease. Allopathy is the exact opposite. Allopathy uses treatments that produce the opposite effects of the symptoms of an illness. The term is currently used to describe modern medicine in developed countries.

Although popular news will make you think that allopathic medicine is the holy grail of medicine, more people are discovering that it isn't. Many people, from medical personnel to patients and their families, are beginning to look to other forms of healthcare, such as alternative medicine.

Medicine From Different Cultures

Modern healthcare in the United States ranks thirty-seventh in the world, among all industrial nations.[4] If we look at U.S. healthcare relative to other cultures, it becomes apparent that they are more effective at managing health, both medically and medicinally.

Many cultures have their own natural remedies, originating in ancient times with the shamans who were either healers or heads of tribes. Many of the medications that were used in those cultures are more effective at treating acute and chronic illnesses. That leads many to speculate that such cultures were much more advanced at healthcare and healing than we may think they were.

There was a time before the advent of patented pharmaceuticals when people did not live as long as they do today, but their quality of life was healthier. This was because the remedies that were used were naturally occurring in the earth, like calcium bentonite clay and other earth- and plant-based remedies that our bodies are equipped to absorb and metabolize.

Calcium bentonite clay, a remedy used since the early days of civilization, is one of the most powerful and potent healing agents in the world. Because medical industries and pharmaceutical companies are not motivated to promote natural remedies, you may not know about the healing properties of calcium bentonite clay. That is because it cannot be patented and, therefore, is not backed by big advertising budgets.

You can find information online if you're seeking natural or alternative remedies, with many of the natural and alternative remedies that are very effective and nothing short of miraculous. They cure ailments and improve health better than many mainstream orthodox medicines. Yet, you certainly will not hear about most of them in mainstream media or medical journals, because that's not what the prevailing healthcare model wants you to use. After all, there's not much money to be made from alternative or natural remedies.

Calcium bentonite clay is curative. It is the only natural remedy I have heard of that can heal a brown recluse spider bite.[7] We find it in many products like Tums or Rolaids. It can significantly improve acne and reduce inflammation, and it adsorbs positively charged ions in the body and systemically flushes toxins. It can be used topically or internally and has even been shown to heal leaky gut syndrome. Even the Bible contains stories of miraculous healings Jesus performed with calcium bentonite clay.

The use of pure, unadulterated turpentine—in this case, the gum scraped from pine trees—as a natural healing remedy is another example of how Earth naturally and abundantly provides for our healing.[8] While the mere idea of using turpentine as medicine may seem disgusting to you, consider that pine spirits have an uncanny ability to restore health and prevent illness by killing off harmful bacteria. Enslaved peoples in Early America commonly used turpentine, and up to this day, those who know about its restorative health properties still use it.

Despite their poor living conditions, enslaved people stayed healthy through their regular use of turpentine. It is enormously curative and was successfully used to treat autoimmune disorders, cancers, and other illnesses.

The Merck Manual, which used to be the bible of medical healthcare, prescribed turpentine and calcium bentonite clay routinely because of their known effectiveness.

However, before you decide that turpentine is the appropriate treatment for you, I urge you to exercise caution: Despite its healing properties, it can be dangerous. ***Do not*** use this remedy without the explicit instructions of a knowledgeable and credentialed healthcare provider. To learn more about this powerful natural remedy, check out the work of Ivy-League-trained physician and healer, Dr. Jennifer Daniels.

Once pharmaceutical companies began to patent medications, many of the commonly used natural remedies up to that point in history, like turpentine and baking soda, became the targets of negative lobbying efforts. The medical community literally removed all references to natural remedies from the Merck Manual at that time because continuing to promote them would not be profitable. As advanced as our U.S. technology is, we seem to have gone backward in the evolution of our own healthcare relative to other cultures and the use of natural remedies.

We can find another example of natural medicines in the Bach flower remedies. Bach was a scientist who discovered floral essences and the energy of highly medicinal flowers. I was introduced to these remedies many years ago as a means of relieving acute stress. You can find them in health stores, but there is little information about the Bach flower remedies from the broader market, presumably because they can't be patented.

Essential oils have remarkable healing properties as well. Thankfully, these remedies are more widely recognized as viable medicinal products and are widely used to supplement conventional healthcare treatments and as standalone remedies.

Frankincense, one such powerful essential oil, is frequently used in cancer treatment even today. You won't see that claim in an advertisement though. It isn't a treatment option endorsed by large pharmaceuticals or the medical community, which depends on you to spend your money, sometimes sacrificing your health, using their chemotherapy drugs or radiation to treat your cancerous cells.

If you're curious about energy healing for cancers, I invite you to go online and search for the use of the ancient art of medical qigong, or the countless evidence-based cures for cancer from the use of Reiki. I have seen live videos of cancerous tumors rapidly and progressively disappearing while being treated by qigong energy healers.

Culturally, our healthcare can be described as archaic. If you were to ask a group of self-respecting oncologists whether they would proceed with chemotherapy and radiation as the first line of intervention to treat their cancer, I can almost certainly guarantee that they would have to carefully weigh the actual effectiveness and impact of the treatment plan against the potential for long-term, irreversible collateral damage. Chemotherapy and radiation are the primary options available for cancer treatment in the mainstream healthcare system, but they are not the only options or the safest options.

Natural remedies have been used to treat cancers long before chemotherapy drugs became the go-to treatment. A good starting point, if you're interested in learning about more natural and effective means for treating cancer, would be to simply do an online search for natural remedies for the treatment of cancer.

The Beginnings of Modern Medicine: Hippocrates

Hippocrates, born around 560 BCE, is known as the father of modern medicine. He is probably the best-known early proponent of the art of healing the body from the inside out. The healing principles he espoused still hold true today. A famous saying of his is, "Let food be your medicine, and let your medicine be food."

Most of the healthcare crisis today can be traced back to what we eat, or the lack of nutrition in today's *Frankenfoods*. These are foods genetically modified with ingredients specifically designed to promote food addiction, enhance flavor, and preserve what they refer to as *freshness*. Go online and check out the fourteen-year-old McDonald's cheeseburger that still looks like it just came off the grill, or the decades-old Twinkie that appears to have just been unwrapped, and you'll get an idea of what preservatives can do. It's creepy, really.

Consequent to the proliferation of chemically engineered foods, we see a whole host of mental and physical health problems that are a direct result of our modern-day diet. This is not a new revelation. In fact, the American Psychiatric Association formed a separate division in the 1950s, focused explicitly on psychiatric disorders and allergies. More people are getting sick today with immunological disorders, cancers, and other lifestyle diseases as a direct result of our food.

The worldwide food market is awash with foods that are not real food anymore. They are full of growth hormones, pesticides, herbicides, fungicides, antibiotics and even prescription drugs, including Prozac. If we would listen to Hippocrates and let food be our medicine—by that I mean real food, not genetically modified food—we would see a reversal in both acute and chronic health issues, including many supposed psychiatric disorders.

These days, everyone knows someone with a food allergy or sensitivity. Our bodies are quite remarkable, but they weren't designed to metabolize anything synthetic over the long term. So, our bodies do their very best to adapt and cope until our immune systems finally get overwhelmed and start to break down.

The Current State of Medicine

The future of medicine, at least in the United States, is pretty scary, to say the least. We don't have a *healthcare* system; we have a *disease*-care system, and it appears to me to be profit-driven, not care-driven, or patient-driven. According to an article published by Karger.com, "There is no treatment that can cure degenerative diseases, but we have many symptomatic treatments." And, as published on medicinenet.com, "by the definition of the U.S. National Center for Health Statistics, chronic diseases generally cannot be prevented by vaccines or cured by medication." Karger further states that, "Improving the quality of life for people with chronic conditions is not possible."[9]

In 1983, the U.S. Congress Office of Technology reported that only 10–20 percent of all procedures in medical practice had been shown scientifically to be effective.[10]

If you need acute care, such as a medically necessary surgery or perhaps to address a broken arm or an acute infection, Western medicine does a decent job of stabilizing your situation. Where it falls short is in the preventing and treating of disease, because the standard of care is to prescribe medications that mask the problem instead of resolving the root cause.

An increasingly alarming phenomenon is the rate of addictions and deaths resulting from prescription medications. I read an article in the American Association of Retired Persons (AARP) monthly magazine that reported that deaths related to overdosing on prescription pain medications rose 700 percent in 2015, up from the previous year. We are a medical culture of over-prescribers. And believe it or not, most patients in our healthcare system get the same treatment plans. It's no wonder one of the leading causes of death in our country is due to medical mistakes.[11]

So the current, and likely future state of healthcare in our country is abominable. It has been estimated that within the next five to ten years, autism rates are expected to rise to a rate of one in two births because of our lifestyles and the prevailing medical model.[12]

The future of medicine is bleak unless we turn it around. With education and training, and as more individuals learn to advocate for better healthcare services and start taking ownership of their own health, we can begin to live happier, healthier lives. It's encouraging to know that there is a growing number of individual providers and health advocates who truly understand the need to practice medicine and healthcare differently.

The current healthcare mandate—unspoken and unwritten, of course—is something I have often heard referred to as *population management.*

I recall logging into our electronic healthcare records software system a few years back, and at the top of the welcome page was the following, spelled out in bold letters:

Welcome to Population Management

I will let you decide what that means, but I can tell you with the world population at approximately 7.7 billion people, the agenda is not on managing or reversing chronic health issues.[13]

As mentioned earlier, the medical industry is profit-driven, not care-driven or prevention-driven. It is not focused on finding or treating the root cause of our current health issues, although we know that our current problems are a result of our lifestyles;

overuse of prescription medications; and misinformation about how to effectively treat health issues. The current medical industry does indeed benefit when symptoms persist, and people die, as shocking as that is.

Healthcare in the United States ranks last among all peer nations in quality of life, and we have the highest infant mortality rate among other industrialized countries.[14] The reason is that the root causes of acute and chronic health issues are not being addressed or treated correctly. If we focused on prevention and cure, pharmaceutical companies and the American Medical Association would not see as much profit as they currently do. The future is somber unless we take a more functional medicinal approach—which, thankfully, many of us in healthcare are now doing.

I am hopeful that growing numbers of healthcare providers are waking up to the reality that people are getting sicker. To change that trend, we need to return to a more natural, functional medicine approach and view healthcare through a holistic, integrative lens. The Earth naturally provides everything we need to heal our minds and bodies. When we focus on stress reduction, moving our bodies, eating healthy plant-based whole foods, and feeding our souls to deepen our connections, we will see the tipping point of a revolution in healthcare and humanity.

The Danger of Allopathic Medicine

Did you know that almost sixty billion dollars are spent just to *market* pharmaceutical drugs each year?[15]

It's essential to know about allopathic medicine so you can make an informed decision when your doctor prescribes medication for you:

- Is the medication prescribed right for you?

- Is it appropriate for your symptoms?

- What are the potential risks and side effects?

- Are there other—more effective or safer—options available?

Allopathic medicines are not your only choice.

Remember that healthcare is not patient-centered; it's profit-driven. Once you're prescribed a medication, mainly if it's prescribed for a chronic condition, you'll likely remain on that medication for the rest of your life.

Statin medications, for example, are the most commonly prescribed cholesterol medications, and once you're on them, the expectation is that you'll be on them forever.

Want to know the truth about cholesterol?

The truth is that cholesterol is a potent antioxidant. It has anti-inflammatory properties. Cholesterol is necessary for our bodies, and we can't live without it. Our bodies produce higher levels of cholesterol in response to a need. Most of our cholesterol is produced in the liver. It's a lipoprotein. Our body secretes LDL cholesterol as a *carrier* to transport cholesterol to an area that needs attention, such as an inflamed vessel. When the affected area has had enough, the HDL cholesterol carries the remainder of the cholesterol back to your liver to be metabolized.

This may surprise you. In 1995, the *Journal of the American Medical Association* showed that there is no evidence linking high cholesterol in women with heart disease. In the Lipitor Study, which had the largest number of men participants studied, the result showed only a 1 percent difference in men who took Lipitor compared to those who took a sugar pill. And, if you're taking a statin, you will have side effects 100 percent of the time.

If you're currently using a statin medication to prevent heart disease, you better question why, because there's no evidence to support that those medications prevent heart disease.

Now, let me be perfectly clear. I'm not your physician, I'm not a medical doctor, I don't diagnose medical conditions, nor am I prescribing anything to you. If you want to review your medications and treatments, I suggest that you talk to your healthcare provider. If you want a doctor who specializes in functional medicine, you can visit IFM.org for a list of licensed and credentialed physicians near you. My intention is to educate you about your options to live a healthier life, not to diagnose your condition or prescribe a treatment option.

In certain acute situations, conventional allopathic prescription medications can work well. For instance, if you have a severe infection, an antibiotic or antifungal may be indicated. But most health issues we are dealing with in our country aren't acute needs. We are primarily dealing with chronic healthcare needs. Allopathic medicines, prescription medicines, and traditional healthcare conventions just don't work most of the time for most of our chronic healthcare needs. That is why people are getting sicker and sicker. We may be living longer, but most people certainly aren't healthier.

Why Allopathic Medicine Fails Most People

I believe most of our population in the United States and abroad have been misinformed about the actual effectiveness of most prescription medications, and the severity and rate of side effects associated with those medications. Every year, billions of dollars are spent by pharmaceutical companies on advertising and marketing. There are powerful lobbyists employed by large pharmaceutical and insurance companies, and the food industry, as well as medical associations, and they spend billions of dollars yearly to figure out new ways to keep us dependent on medications that either don't work or will cause more harm than good.

The message that most people hear is precisely the message that pharmaceutical companies want people to hear. It seems like we can't get through a television show these days without seeing a commercial for prescription medication. Traditional allopathic medical models and leaders in medicine are less likely to focus on natural remedies, such as stress reduction or anti-inflammatory foods, as natural healers of cancer.

There is a much bigger agenda at work here. Mainstream doctors and healthcare providers are well-meaning, but they have been duped, too.

For example, guess who writes and sponsors the medical school curriculum? If you guessed medical associations or some governmental organizations, you'd be wrong.

Large pharmaceuticals do.[16] They have been sponsoring the content taught in medical schools for decades, and well-meaning doctors are simply educating their patients based on what they have learned. Their education is based primarily on pharmaceutical and medical inventions, which are biased and, sometimes, not even based on evidence.

Oh, they may not be necessarily wrong, but they definitely don't tell the whole story, and when it comes to health and healthcare, a partial truth may be worse than a lie.

Look at depression, for example. How many prescriptions do you think are written for antidepressant medications in a given year?

The fact is, many antidepressant medications don't fare well when compared to placebos.[17] When we compare the effectiveness of antidepressants to exercise in a study, after thirty days, the efficacy and benefits of exercise far outperform those of antidepressant medications, and there are no adverse side effects with exercise. There are, however, potential risks with any kind of exercise, so I recommend you consult with your physician first to see if you are able to undertake a certain program.

Why aren't more doctors prescribing exercise as a treatment for depression?

I'm sure it comes as no surprise that there is misinformation and miseducation regarding health and healthcare. The prevailing trends in healthcare are not focused on people being healthy. If they were, our advertising dollars would be spent on educating people about prevention and cure. There is more money spent on marketing than research and development.

For example, one pharmaceutical company spent nearly $60 million on marketing their drugs, while its research and development budget was only $31 million in comparison.

We have been led to believe that the healthcare provider is the expert and that they know best, but that typical practitioner only knows what the pharmaceutical companies have influenced to be taught in many medical schools. Although many new medical professionals are concerned enough to invest in additional education about alternative options and to share it with their patients, they are only an exception, the minority. And so, we sit on the edge of a dangerous tipping point for the U.S. healthcare crisis.

What Risks Are Posed by Allopathic Medicine?

As found on desispeaks.com:

> Modern Medicine, through over-prescription, represents a major threat to public health. Peter Gøtzsche, co-founder of the reputed Cochrane Collaboration, estimates that prescribed medication is the third-most common cause of death globally after heart disease and cancer.

In the UK, the use of prescription drugs is at an all-time high, with almost half of adults on at least one drug, and one-quarter of them on three. This is an increase of 47% in the past decade. It's instructive to note that life expectancy in the UK has stalled since 2010, the slowdown being the most significant in the world's leading economies.[18]

A Time and Place for Allopathic Medicine

If you have an acute fever or an infection, allopathic medicine can work exceptionally well. A broad-spectrum antibiotic can be effective in curing the infection. If you break your leg and need a cast, or you need surgery to repair injuries sustained in an accident, allopathic medicine is the logical and best option for this type of acute situation. There's a time and a place for all forms of healing, including traditional allopathic medicine. It's important to discern which kind of healing is the best option for each specific situation.

What I'm advocating is a system in which all parties concerned in the healthcare of a sick patient are active participants in the treatment.

Functional Medicine

To stay healthy, you want to follow the functional medicine approach. It is an approach based on biological systems and is more concerned with restoring optimal health and wellness rather than just curing diseases.

This model focuses on a balanced lifestyle, including:

- Getting proper rest

- Healthy nutrition

- Reducing inflammation

- Managing and reducing stress

- Rebalancing hormones

Focusing on these elements is a highly effective approach to understanding and reversing chronic conditions. This model is becoming more prevalent with each passing day.

In a functional medicine model, the client or patient is an active participant in their own care. Treatment is a team approach, and it's the only approach in modern medicine that can effectively treat and often reverse the chronic degenerative disease states that exist today—heart disease, diabetes, most cancers, most immune disorders, and most psychiatric disorders.

The functional medicine model offers a solution to these health problems by adopting Hippocrates' prescription for healthy food and creating healthier lifestyles.

Our bodies and minds know how to heal themselves. The major problem is that we interfere with that process and cause untold damage to our systems. To ensure that we remain healthy, we can help our bodies and minds heal and further stay healthy through:

- Healthy nutrition

- Proper rest

- Feeding our minds and souls in ways that nurture, not undermine

- Developing healthier relationships with ourselves and others

- Managing and reducing stress

- Getting the right kind of exercise

I invite you to read more about foods and moods. Search online and read some of the available evidence-based literature. Simply type in the phrase "how foods affect moods" and read some of the available evidence-based literature.

It is known that symptoms of many diseases, disorders, or conditions such as those listed below can be totally remediated by healing our gut microbiome and fortifying our bodies through nutrient therapy:[19]

- Autism

- Schizophrenia

- Depression

- Anxiety

For example, when we remove gluten, sugars, and dairy from our diets, in most cases, we see mental and physical health issues completely reversed or halted in their tracks; at the very least, the conditions can be better managed when those foods are no longer ingested. Again, the solution is to return to Hippocrates' model and let food be our medicine.

IF HEALTHCARE IS SO ADVANCED, WHY DO THE SICK KEEP GETTING SICKER?

Wake up now and take control of your health. The only way to lead a healthy, fully satisfying life is to understand your options, move away from spoon-fed marketing and advertising messages, and take responsibility for your personal health. That includes education, understanding the research, knowing the current state of the healthcare environment, and being aware of whose agenda is determining your path so you can make an informed decision to take control of your health and the health of your family.

We teach our children our lifestyle habits, and they teach their children their lifestyle habits, and the cycle goes on. If those lifestyle habits are based upon misinformation, then generations after generations are at risk.

An Ounce of Prevention Is Worth a Pound of Cure

We spend more money on healthcare than any other industrialized nation, yet we are one of the sickest nations in the world. It may surprise you to know that 65 percent of Americans are obese or overweight. Seventy-five percent of all healthcare costs are spent on preventable diseases, which are the significant causes of death and disability. The big lifestyle diseases are diabetes, cancer, heart disease, and immune disorders. If we focus on prevention, we can save billions of dollars in healthcare costs and start reclaiming our health.

Some simple preventive techniques come back to the functional medicine model: eat clean, healthy, live foods. "Live foods" are foods that are dense with nutrients.

Make it a point to get between seven and eight hours of sleep every night. The most crucial rest you get is when you go to sleep before midnight. Every hour of sleep you get before midnight is worth two hours of sleep in terms of healing and restoration.[20]

Next, our bodies are meant to be in motion. Move your body. Get up and go for a walk. Exercise. Practice yoga. Swim. Find something that you enjoy and stick with it.

You also need to address stress management. It seems that there are more mental, emotional, and time demands placed on us now compared to any other time in the history of humanity. One contributing factor to illness and disease is inflammation, and one of the significant causes of inflammation, besides our dietary intake, is stress.

Find ways to reduce and manage stress through any of these methods:

- Meditating
- Laughing
- Sloppy-wet kisses from your dog
- Hanging out with friends
- Watching funny movies
- Prayer
- Deep breathing
- Gardening
- Reading

All these are simple strategies that move us toward prevention and wellness. If you're not focused on prevention, you are likely going to get sicker and sicker, and you are going to spend more and more of your money chasing after healthcare interventions that simply don't work. Americans spend more than 11 percent of *pre-tax* dollars on healthcare.[21]

That doesn't include after-tax dollars. An ounce of prevention really *is* worth a pound of cure, especially if you want to live a life of wellness and vitality. It won't happen, though, unless you are focused on prevention.

Truth, Lies, and Marketing

It's a bold statement, but most of the information available about health and our food is misinformation. Marketers target our fears and our vanity. It's easy to influence people when they are stressed and fearful.

Advertisers focus their messages to tap into three main areas of our psyche, related to:

1. Survival needs, such as food, clothing, and shelter

2. Sex and sex appeal

3. Acceptance and belonging needs

Every successful marketing or advertising campaign appeals consciously or unconsciously to one or more of these innate needs. That's one of the reasons I often recommend that people minimize their exposure to the news and commercials—they're bad for your health. Most news reports are focused on reporting negative information, which causes us stress, which in turn makes us easy prey for marketers.

Without saying they are outright lying, it's well known that in the healthcare industry, research studies and outcomes can be easily manipulated, depending on how you calculate and interpret the statistics and how you spin that information. The Lipitor study that I referred to earlier is a prime example.

How many billions of dollars are made each year from selling and prescribing statins because people are scared into believing that they will have a heart attack if they don't take the medications?

Marketing pharmaceuticals accounts for 3 percent of our total U.S. healthcare spending. According to *Forbes* magazine, it's estimated that we spend more than $3.8 trillion on healthcare every year, which is disturbing.[22]

The truth is that most prescription medications aren't statistically significant in terms of the benefits outweighing the risks. With prescription medicines, there are far more risks than benefits to the individual. Again, there is a time and a place for prescription medications, and some people do well on certain medicines. Still, honestly, those medications should be reserved for acute and temporary situations while actively seeking to identify and remediate the exact underlying causes of the disorder or disease. Most medication use can be avoided by focusing on prevention, including making healthy lifestyle changes.

If medications indeed were the answer, don't you think Americans would be getting healthier, not sicker?

Americans spend twice as much on healthcare compared to all other countries, yet our lifespan isn't even in the top twenty among industrial nations. People are getting sicker because their bodies weren't designed to metabolize and break down *synthetic* anything. We can do it for a while and be okay, but throughout long-term treatments, our bodies start to break down because they can't tolerate synthetic pharmaceuticals.

Due to misuse and over-prescription of allopathic medications, there is potential for adverse interaction effects of each medicine. In most cases, when people are on four, five, or more drugs, there is usually a negative interaction effect, meaning that the drugs don't mix well together, and the combinations can be unpredictable and, in some cases, lethal. Physicians may fail to take into account the potential risks associated with what's called *polypharmacy*, taking multiple medications together.

Healthcare providers may be too distracted to note interactions, or the medications may be prescribed by different specialists who do not communicate with each other. Because doctors are often compensated based on production, they may not take the time to review the medication interaction effects or check in with their patients to be sure they are aware of all prescription drugs their patients are taking.

Your pharmacist can be a great resource to notice the potential for medication interaction effects. It is also true, in my clinical and personal experience, that many pharmacists are anxious about telling patients directly that some medications should not be taken together. It appears they are afraid of stepping on the prescribing physician's toes, so to speak.

Americans spend five hundred billion dollars annually on prescription drugs. That is just in the United States, and that is three hundred billion dollars more annually than the rest of the world spends, at least. We are the most expensive country in terms of healthcare costs, and our healthcare is the least effective.

Have We Been Duped? The Heart of the Matter: Root Cause Rather Than Symptom Management

If we really want to focus on wellness, health, and vitality, we need to focus our interventions on understanding the root cause of simple illnesses. The heart of the matter where good health and wellness are concerned dictates that we need to educate people about the origins of disease. That is why I am excited to share some of my thoughts with you in this book.

Healthcare providers are increasingly focusing on the root cause. This leads us back to integrative medicines that highlight lifestyle function, movement, detoxification, clean, healthy foods, spiritual practices, and stress management. Symptom management clearly does not work for reasons stated earlier.

When we focus on only managing symptoms through pharmaceuticals, more often than not, we create additional complications. For example, it's kind of scary to realize that we have been taught to believe that a hospital is where we can go to get better, yet many people don't get better when they are hospitalized. There is a time and a place for acute treatment centers such as hospitals. We need hospitals for certain situations, but we also see people dying needlessly from the care they've received while hospitalized.

Upon my mother's discharge from a recent hospitalization, she was prescribed the same pain medication, in generic and brand name forms, by three different doctors attending to her, at three different doses, and told to take as prescribed. My mom, being a good patient, followed doctors' orders, and nearly died from an overdose of pain medications shortly after she was released from the hospital. In a short period, she developed congestive heart failure as a result and died. We frequently see this with the elderly.

The number of people who die from such complications is alarming.

When we are only paying attention to symptoms, it's like putting a Band-Aid on an infectious disease. It simply is not going to have a lasting impact. It may mask an outward sore, but your body will continue to be ravaged by the underlying cause.

To only manage symptoms does not improve health. That is why our healthcare system is the least effective among industrialized nations. Its primary focus is on symptom management, not identifying and successfully resolving the underlying root cause of the problem.

When the focus is on the root cause, people can actually get better. I encourage more healthcare professionals, who are reshaping their interventions and their practice styles, to look for and understand the underlying root cause of their patients' illnesses.

In most cases, the root cause of the illness is some sort of inflammation. Natural ways to reduce inflammation— including integrative and functional medicine, which may involve the use of antioxidant-rich foods, clean water, exercise, or stress reduction—can not only alleviate peoples' symptoms, but often completely remediate health issues. The only way people can genuinely reclaim their health is by understanding and focusing on proper interventions for the root cause.

This is a hopeful message. As people become more educated and make proactive decisions to take control of and advocate for their health, better outcomes will emerge. In my clinical experience, patients who advocate for their health—meaning they take ownership of their health and don't hesitate to question their healthcare providers—will have the greatest success.

CHAPTER 2

WHAT IS INTEGRATIVE HEALTH AND WELLNESS?

Under what we have seen as the failings of traditional allopathic medicine, there is a need for a drastic change in how we manage health and healthcare. Simply prescribing a whole slew of drugs will not solve the issue. Instead, medical practitioners, patients, and other involved parties need to approach the problem of healthcare from an entirely different angle.

One of the ways that we can accomplish this is by the use of the Integrative Healthcare Model.

What Is Integrative Healthcare?

Integrative healthcare is an approach to healthcare that attempts to integrate the best of Western or traditional scientific medicine with a broader understanding of the nature of illnesses, healing, and wellness. It is an attempt to move away from the *disease-free* standard of allopathic medicine, and toward a much healthier alternative.

As was discussed in the previous chapter, traditional medicine is more of a *disease-care* centered approach than a *healthcare* one. In other words, under conventional Western medicine, the medical practitioner is more concerned with diagnosing a patient with a known disease, and they prescribe a medication, drug, or treatment to such a patient without considering it in the broader context of that patient's physical, emotional, and spiritual health.

Integrative Healthcare is a holistic approach to healthcare that puts the patient as the primary subject of the care. It considers and addresses the full range of physical, spiritual, mental, social, emotional, and environmental influences that can affect the health of such a patient. The Integrative Healthcare Model goes beyond simply prescribing medication for the person willy-nilly to treating the whole being. It means addressing both the patient's immediate and long-term needs as well as the complex interaction of a range of biological, psychosocial, behavioral, and environmental factors.

This process helps patients to recover from illnesses. But much more than that, it helps them to remain healthy, which is more than can be said about allopathic medicine. The core principles on which integrative medicine is built are as follows:

- The medical practitioner and patient are partners, working together to accomplish the healing process.

- The factors that affect disease, health, and wellness are all considered.

- The care provided affects the whole person—including the body, mind, and spirit—in the broader context of the community.

- Healthcare providers use many healing sciences, both traditional and alternative, to stimulate and accelerate the human body's natural healing response.

- Whenever possible, integrative practitioners use natural and less invasive interventions that are proven effective.

- The Integrative Healthcare Model is scientifically based, as all functional medicine is, and as such, is driven by inquiry and is open to newer and better forms of care provision.

- In addition to treatment, promoting good health and wellness, as well as the prevention of diseases, is essential.

- Care is highly individualized to address the patient's conditions as best as possible. It takes into account the unique needs, circumstances, and health requirements of the patient.

While integrative healthcare is the sum of a set of principles and mentalities on how to handle healthcare as a whole, integrative medicine is a narrower discipline that is more concerned with the process and actual practice of the principles of the Integrative Healthcare Model.

These principles are foundational to integrative health and wellness and reflect my approach to healthy living. The critical distinction to keep in mind is that integrative health and wellness encompasses a person's whole health: body, mind, and spirit.

Integrative Medicine

Integrative medicine is rooted in the definition of health. Health is defined by the World Health Organization (WHO) as "a state of complete physical, mental and social well-being, and not merely the absence of disease or infirmity."[23] Interestingly, this definition in and of itself should disqualify the traditional allopathic healthcare model because, at its heart, conventional medicine is mostly concerned with eliminating or managing diseases and doesn't even do that job well.

Integrative Medicine looks to restore and maintain a high standard of health and wellness throughout a person's lifetime by gaining an understanding of the patient's unique circumstances, considering the mental, spiritual, physical, social, and environmental factors that influence the patient's health. By personalizing healthcare, integrative medicine treats all the possible causes of an illness, as well as any related factors, rather than merely treating symptoms. Integrative medicine is not the same as alternative medicine, which seeks to replace allopathic medicine techniques. Preferably, integrative medicine can, and will, often include allopathic medicine techniques. The primary distinguishing feature, though, is that the patient and their family are all active participants in the treatment, and other methods of treatment are willingly explored in the context of a patient's situation rather than a *one-size-fits-all* approach that traditional Western medicine would propose.

Integrative health and wellness practitioners view people as the unity of mind, body, and spirit and the systems in which they live. There is a focus on prevention and treatment. Providers promote health; they prevent illness and raise awareness of diseases and healthy lifestyles rather than merely managing symptoms. An integrative holistic approach relieves symptoms, modifies contributing factors, and enhances the client's life system to optimize future well-being. There is a focus on innate healing power. Humans are designed with these fantastic inherent healing abilities. Research in quantum physics explores the extent of these abilities. Holistic health and wellness practitioners evoke, educate, and help clients utilize these powers to affect the healing process.

The Principles of Health and Wellness, approved by the Academy of Integrative Health & Medicine, include:

> Optimal health is the goal of holistic practice. It is the conscious pursuit of the highest level of functioning and balance of the physical, environmental, mental, emotional, social, and spiritual aspects of human experience, resulting in a dynamic state of being fully alive. This creates a condition of well well-being regardless of the presence or absence of disease or other life challenges. . . . Holistic health care practitioners strive to meet the client with grace, kindness, acceptance, and spirit without condition, as love is life's most powerful healer.[24]

THE HISTORY OF INTEGRATIVE HEALTH AND WELLNESS

You must know the history of integrative health and wellness, so you are equipped to make informed health decisions that are in your highest and best interests. The pioneers in this field of medicine worked diligently to expose progressive options for healthy living and disease prevention that would save future generations from making old mistakes. I am grateful and happy to share what I've learned from them.

Where Did Integrative Medicine Come From?

Integrative medicine got its start in the United States during the 1960s during the counterculture movement, grew through the new age movement of the 1970s, and gained more traction in the 1980s. Early pioneers were Dr. Andrew Weil and Dr. Bernie Siegel, physicians and authors who look beyond the barriers of traditional medicine to find alternative approaches that directly involve patients in their own care.

Physicians in the United States became increasingly interested in taking alternative approaches to their medical practices. By 1995, 80 percent of practicing family physicians took an interest in receiving training in acupuncture, hypnotherapy, and massage therapy. These modalities have been used for millennia to induce healing. In the mid-1990s, hospitals in the United States began to open associated integrative medicine clinics. For example, The Consortium of Academic Health Centers for Integrative Medicine was founded in 1999 to focus on understanding integrative approaches to health and healing, and by 2015, it included sixty members.

In 1991, the U.S. government established the Office of Alternative Medicine—now known as the National Center for Complementary and Alternative Medicine, to explore the use of alternative medicine treatments. Their mission is to define, through rigorous scientific investigation, the usefulness and safety of complementary and integrative health interventions and their roles in improving health and healthcare.[25]

The Academic Consortium for Integrative Medicine and Health has developed the following definition for integrative medicine and health:

> Integrative medicine and health reaffirms the importance of the relationship between practitioner and patient, focuses on the whole person, is informed by evidence, and makes use of all appropriate therapeutic and lifestyle approaches, healthcare professionals, and disciplines to achieve optimal health and healing.[26]

Proponents say integrative medicine is not the same as complementary and alternative medicine (CAM), nor is it merely the combination of conventional medicine with complementary and alternative medicine. Instead of that, they say that it "emphasizes wellness and healing of the entire person (bio-psycho-socio-spiritual dimensions) as primary goals, drawing on both conventional and CAM approaches in the context of a supportive and effective physician patient relationship."

We are now at a place where proponents of integrative medicine say the impetus for the adoption of integrative medicine stems in part from an increasing percentage of the population who consult complementary medicine practitioners. Patients are increasingly unsatisfied with conventional medicine and what they perceive as a focus on using pharmaceuticals to treat or suppress a specific disease rather than helping a patient or client become healthy. They take the view that it is essential to go beyond the particular complaint and draw upon a combination of conventional and alternative approaches to help create a state of health that is more than the absence of disease. Proponents further suggest that physicians have become so specialized that the traditional role of a comprehensive health-giver who focuses on healing and wellness has been neglected.[27]

I strongly agree with that statement.

Recently in the United States, many more people are focusing on integrative medicine as a potential solution to the healthcare crisis. It provides healthcare that is centered on patients, is healing-oriented, and emphasizes the relationship between therapeutic approach and its uses that originated from conventional and alternative medicine (CAM). The lifestyle changes undertaken in this model are gradually being recognized as a strategy to defeat the epidemic of chronic illnesses ruining many lives and bankrupting the economy. A lot of proponents suggest that a model for the integrative healthcare system should be grounded in a team-based approach, with a primary health partner who knows the patient and their loved ones, as well as the unique circumstances surrounding the patient. And as such, it can address the bodily, mental, and spiritual needs of the patient. The primary partner provides care under this model, with a whole team of specialists who are at the centerpiece of this health-giving and restorative process, which is then presented to the patient, with a plan for repairing and restoring health at its optimum level.

For the integrative model of medicine to flourish in the United States, new providers and newer provider models are needed, along with a readjustment of incentives and a commitment to help promote disease management consciousness. As was stated earlier, we are now aware that conventional medicine cannot treat effectively and efficiently 80–90 percent of all chronic degenerative disease processes.[28] The traditional medical model and insurance-based services are leaving more people sick, and they do not necessarily teach people to get healthy or help them remain so.

Where Are We Going?

There is still massive resistance to integrative health and wellness from several places. That includes large pharmaceuticals and the health insurance industry. As we know now, there is big money in healthcare, upward of 3.8 trillion dollars yearly, as we've previously cited.

In March 2016, the DARK Act was voted into law. The DARK Act—so named by opponents as an acronym for *Denying Americans the Right to Know*—is intended to keep the public in the dark about chemically engineered additives in food by negating current food labeling guidelines. Although this was signed into law, there is still much we can do to promote integrative health and wellness. Further progress is in your hands, and you can make a difference by:

- Demanding better care

- Researching centuries-old remedies

- Seeking more information about integrative health and wellness options

- Educating yourself and your family

- Creating a tipping point within the medical community will come with your proactive interest in integrative treatment modalities. Talk with your healthcare provider about your options. Health and wellness are your birthright. Be your own advocate.

Cancer Care: An Integrative Healthcare Example

One example of an area of medicine that combines both Western medicine and other alternative forms of healthcare is cancer treatment. Traditional allopathic treatments—such as surgery, radiation therapy, chemotherapy, and others—are being combined with alternative methods of treatments like acupuncture and meditation to help the patients cope with any side effects of the cancer treatment. Some of the integrative methods of cancer treatment in use include, but are not limited to:

- **Acupuncture**: This practice involves placing needles along the energy fields of the body, called *meridians*, to balance the body's energy.

- **Massage Therapy**: Massages have been found to provide some benefits generally, as well as specific benefits to cancer patients.

- **Meditation**: Clinical trials have studied guided and self-directed meditation and prayer as ways of relaxing and reducing thoughts that interfere with mindfulness.

- **Reiki**: The International Association of Reiki Professionals describes Reiki as "channeling positive energy into your body, with (practitioners) typically placing their hands on the affected areas of your body that need a boost, offering this this energy, and your body takes in the energy where most needed."[29]

- **Yoga**: Yoga has many different types, such as hatha yoga, a more physically focused variant that is the most commonly practiced. It incorporates poses and physical movements to balance the spirit. Medically speaking, yoga does appear to increase energy levels, as well as flexibility, and help reduce pain. It also provides yogis with a sense of calmness and tranquility.

- **Qigong**: This practice uses controlled breathing, movement, and meditation to balance the body's energy.

- **Art and Music Therapy**: Studies have shown that practicing art and playing music may have some positive effect on the health of patients, such as boosting T-cells, a part of the body's immune system that fight cancer.

At first glance, these rather unorthodox methods may seem unusual, and even frivolous to you. However, it would be reasonable for you stop and consider belief systems. How much of them are influenced by the lies and misinformation you've accepted from biased marketing?

You must remember that the goal of integrative medicine is to select a treatment, or series of procedures, that restores a particular patient to an optimum level of health, considering that individual patient's circumstances. In other words, a combination of some techniques above may work for one patient, while a totally separate combination will work for another patient, even if both have a similar sickness.

Ordinarily, this would be a cause for concern under the traditional Western medical approach, since it focuses only on the disease. With the focus on the patient, though—the understanding that each patient is a separate individual and that no two cases are exactly the same—the integrative approach is comprehensive and even accepts that treatments for patients will differ, even if their symptoms or illnesses are the same.

BIOLOGICAL IMPERATIVES

Although humans are spiritual beings, our physical presence on Earth requires that we fulfill basic needs—*biological imperatives*—to survive and thrive.

There are three main biological imperatives:

1. Survival: food, clothing, shelter, and money

2. Belonging and affiliation

3. Sex

Survival: Food, Clothing, Shelter, and Money

The most underdeveloped places on Earth tend to be the places with the highest levels of disease, sickness, and health-related deaths. More-developed nations of the world rank quite high on the modern healthcare list. It is logical and stands to reason, after all, that you can't live in a state of health and wellness if your basic needs for survival—food, clothing, shelter, and money—are not being met. If you are cold, have no home, and struggle to eat every day, your health may not feel like a priority. If you have no money to meet your basic needs, your daily existence will be stressful. Stress diminishes your physical health, and thus ensues a vicious cycle that undermines your whole health.

The absence of any of these three survival needs is what we call *poverty*, and it's tough to handle. Statistically speaking, poverty is the most significant cause of poor health in the United States.[30] Similarly, sociodemographics show that "in both races and regions, individuals with lower income and education had higher rates of chronic disease and unhealthy behaviors than those with higher income and education."[31] This is double the number seen among those who aren't poor. That's scary.

Again, the rates of avoidable visits and stays in hospitals are highest in more impoverished neighborhoods.[32] This factor is worsened by the *prescription medication* mentality of modern medicine. After all, if a diabetic, for example, cannot afford the diet prescribed by the doctor or nutritionist, it becomes harder to manage the illness. And if a patient is struggling for a long period of time, as perhaps a single mother whose rent is long overdue would be, then the stress may eventually cause heart problems.

Of course, the patient probably would not be able to afford the kind of healthcare that would enable them to manage the sickness, and so the cycle continues.

Let me use my story as an example. I was the youngest of ten kids born to a single mom; our dad abandoned us before my birth. Our family couldn't focus on health and wellness, spirituality, or independence, much less on higher education. Every effort was directed to meeting our basic needs for food, clothing, and shelter. We worked hard. Even then, the threat of eviction loomed over us.

Thankfully, our situation improved in time. To learn more about my personal story, check out my first Harvard presentation, which you can find on my website, thecifhw.com, or on our YouTube video channel, youtu.be/vBH-b8uXoh8.

It speaks directly to the importance of meeting basic needs first. It also demonstrates how to live fully in body, mind, and spirit with the right information and mentoring to support you. I hope it inspires you.

As another example, the standard medical procedure would have any practitioner work to keep a patient's blood pressure and blood sugar down. But what can be done in a situation where the patient has unpaid bills mounting up, lives in a violent neighborhood, and is under threat of eviction?

I have worked with many primary care providers who say when basic needs are unmet, such as in cases of substandard housing, inadequate nutrition, loneliness, and a lack of opportunities economically, health and wellness suffer.

As a result of this, many healthcare institutions are turning to more integrative methods of healthcare, which are focused on treating each patient's case uniquely. For example, some hospitals pay for meals to be home delivered as a way to reduce and prevent admissions in hospitals.

Nonetheless, the best these methods can do is to react to cases where sickness is already present. While it is good to help sick patients get better faster, any expense or treatment that *prevents* patients from getting sick in the first place is more worthwhile.

Thus, we need more social care programs and treatments, rather than strictly healthcare, to provide the fundamental survival imperatives. This will reduce the incidences of illnesses and improve health and wellness.

Belonging and Affiliation

The second biological imperative is belonging and affiliation. Studies have shown that humans are social animals, and we are hardwired to seek social interaction and companionship. As much as popular culture philosophies tout "being your own self" and millennials declare *needing space*, the truth is that we are hardwired to form relationships. Even in the absence of other people, we will establish connections and bonds with animals. Remember the typical lonely cat lady stereotype.

This tendency is probably an evolutionary one because going back to prehistoric times, your chances of survival were higher if you were part of a group, tribe, or family. In those days, food was scarce, with humans competing in a predator-rich environment. There was power in numbers, so the larger the group, the tribe, or the family, the better.

The need for belonging and affiliation seems to have been hardwired in humans from those early times.

Abraham Maslow recognized the importance of belonging and included it in his *hierarchy of needs*, ranking just above the survival imperatives.[33] In his work, the psychologist investigated peoples' motivation and discovered that we are driven to carry out activities that help us meet our needs. In other words, every person has particular needs to be met and will expend time and effort on activities that help meet those needs.

In his hierarchy of needs, which was presented as a pyramid, basic needs filled the bottom and the needs increased in complexity as you ascended the pyramid. At the very base of the pyramid are physiological needs, such as food, shelter, and clothing. In basic terms, these needs must be fulfilled to remain alive. Directly above them is the need for safety, and above that, the need for belonging.

According to Maslow, your lower-order needs must be satisfied before you can focus on higher-order needs.

The need for belonging can, however, be a detriment to well-being if it causes you to act or believe a certain way just to fit in. This happens with young children and adolescents who desperately need to feel connected with their peers and often make poor choices as a result of their need for belonging. Peer pressure is a legitimate issue that your kids grapple with as they grow up.

Adults can also get caught in the cycle of seeking acceptance and approval and end up in abusive relationships or as resentful martyrs who alienate the people they most want to be close to.

Today, humans can survive without being part of a family or having the approval and acceptance of others. However, *thriving* without a sense of belonging is unlikely.

Thriving requires a healthy sense of belonging and affiliation, one of the building blocks for true integrative health and wellness. Feeling like you belong supports you to engage in mutually respectful relationships that contribute to your overall well-being and whole health—body, mind, and spirit.

This means that a healthy sense of community is vital to improved health and wellness. This is another area that integrative health takes into consideration.

Sex

Until recent history, the sexual act was the primary root of human procreation. With the advent of in-vitro fertilization and other assisted reproductive technologies, sex is no longer the only means for procreation. However, it is still a vital biological imperative.

Although you can survive without sex, most experts would agree that it is a meaningful part of a healthy, full, and vital life. Studies have shown that sex is extremely beneficial to our health as it activates a variety of neurotransmitters that impact not only our brains, but several other organs in our bodies.[34]

It is often said that meaningful sex is *the great equalizer*. It reduces stress, helps you sleep better, increases the likelihood of maintaining a stable weight, and keeps your body healthy, among other benefits. Sex is an indispensable element in healthy, intimate relationships.

These biological imperatives—survival needs, belonging and affiliation, and sex—are at the core of your health and wellness. Meeting those needs first gives you the foundation on which to build the other elements of your whole health.

A holistic approach to health and wellness, therefore, needs to include elements that touch all these areas, rather than focusing on only one. An understanding of the complex interplay of these factors leads to a balanced approach of providing healthcare services that restore and maintain optimum health levels.

THE FOUNDATIONS—THE FIVE PILLARS OF HEALTH

You must understand the five pillars of health if you want to transform your body, mind, and life. The five pillars of health create a balanced, whole-health system mentally, emotionally, and physically that allows you to reach your higher order goals of self-actualization. Without understanding and optimizing the five pillars, you cannot truly live your best life.

The five pillars of health are:

1. Detoxifying your body

2. Exercise

3. Social, emotional, and spiritual relationships

4. Nutrition and supplementation

5. Balanced hormones

Detoxifying Your Body

I want to recognize Dr. Charles Webb and his expertise in functional medicine as a trusted source for some of this information. I invite you to read his remarkable book, titled *Metamorphosis*. I'm delighted that this kind of information has become common knowledge. The more you know about how to get healthy and stay healthy, the higher the chance of having a positive impact on everything and everyone in your life.

Living in our modern society, we are exposed to many chemical substances, and we ingest them daily. Almost everywhere you look, products are chemically treated for one reason or the other. Municipal tap water, prescription drugs, health and hygiene products, and additives to processed food, such as flavors, sweeteners, and preservatives, are prime targets for chemical treatment. Electro-Magnetic Radiation—sometimes referred to as EMF, for the electro-magnetic field—from all the technology around us, as well as numerous other factors, contributes to the buildup of inorganic materials in our systems. Unfortunately, our bodies weren't designed to process chemicals and other synthetic products continuously or consistently. Ordinarily, the body can get rid of harmful toxins on its own when it is in small doses. When toxins accumulate, however, our organs work overtime to handle these compounds, and they will inevitably break down eventually.

When this happens, how do we attempt to handle it? You guessed it—if we are following the typical medical model, the answer is more chemicals. To understand this clearer, imagine you get a brand-new car, an extremely durable and well-built one, and then you decide to operate it daily under the harshest of conditions, and at the highest of speeds. Of course, we'll expect it to wear out faster, to need repair, overhauling, and replacement more often than was claimed as the maximum life; it seems to be basic common sense.

It's therefore startling how surprised we act when we hear that our lifestyles are contributing to our ill-health. It's really no wonder the national level of health and wellness is dropping drastically. Your present state of health is a result of exposure to, and accumulation of, toxins stored in the body over a long period.

Accumulated toxins may be a significant root cause of all diseases and bodily dysfunctions, as well as a major part of aging. Some studies have found mitigating health factors make one more prone to contract the COVID-19 virus or less able to fight it off. High toxin levels compromise the body's immune response.[35]

Detoxifying is simply a way of assisting the body to rid harmful toxins that tend to build up and cause sicknesses. Detoxifying is a whole-body process that addresses issues with your nervous system and internal organs that, if left unchecked, can lead to chronic illness.

Getting regular chiropractic adjustments, for example, releases stress on your nerves, allows your body's natural energy channels to flow without undue impediments, and keeps your nervous system operating smoothly.

Approach the detoxifying of your organs and glands—liver, kidneys, gut, and gallbladder—from a nutritional and hormonal perspective. In line with the principles of integrative medicine, detoxifying your body helps prevent ill-health by strengthening your body to do that which it was meant to do in the first place.

It's like spring cleaning for your body. It strips your internal system of buildup of toxins from the environment, stress, inflammation, and genetically modified food, so your body can absorb the nutrients it needs to be healthy.

If you don't detoxify your organs regularly, food will rot in your gut, creating a nasty overgrowth of harmful bacteria. When it gets this bad, even if you can digest your food, your body may be unable to absorb nutrients or break down proteins. If your body cannot break down proteins, you will be unable to metabolize fats. If you can't metabolize fats, you will add weight. This domino effect can set the stage for chronic degenerative disease conditions.

The purpose of detoxification is to reduce and cleanse the buildup of toxins in the body more effectively. Dr. Drew Johnson defines detoxification as:

> A bodily process in which unhealthy toxins are converted into less harmful or harmless substances and are then excreted. The process of detoxification involves attempts in the body to achieve a new level of homeostasis after some positive changes are made in diet or other behaviors. It intends, at least short-term, to relieve stress on the liver and the other excretory organs so they can better function at their job.[36]

When your body is functioning well, it naturally reduces environmental toxins and is better equipped to deal with emotional or mental stress. The buildup of toxins can have negative effects on your body physically. Some of the problems that toxins cause include:

- Digestive problems, such as stomach upset, gas, bloating, and constipation

- Low energy

- PMS

- Headaches

- Irritability

- Depression

- Anxiety

- Chronic aches and pains

- Immune disorders, such as fibromyalgia

- Chronic fatigue

- Arthritis

- Hormonal imbalances

- Weight gain

- High cholesterol

Detoxifying your body not only makes you feel better, but also offers many other behind-the-scenes benefits, including:

- Restoring more normal processes and functions to your body

- Eliminating free radical damage that can accelerate the aging process and potentially cause cancer

- Strengthening your immune system

- Improving your overall health and organ function

- Elevating your mood

- Enhancing your cognitive functions to make learning and recollection easier

- Helping you replace unhealthy habits with restorative, health-renewing habits

The process of detoxification is individual. The type of detox you require is based on your personal health goals, your biological and chemical makeup, and the amount of exposure to toxins that you've had. It is a revolutionary process, one that expands as you improve your health and optimizes the benefits gained.

The major toxins that need to be removed from your body to restore optimal functionality are heavy metals and toxic chemicals. You will also need to remove toxins for chronic infestations (Lyme, mold, Candida, parasites virus), halogens (chlorine, bromine, fluoride), and unwanted accumulation of calcium, among other things.

When detoxifying, you work from the outside in; that is, from the external environment to the internal environment.

First, you may start with an assessment of your oral health. Detoxify the toxins from mercury fillings, jawbone infections, and cavitation, as well as your environment, and then begin to work inward. Next, you can detoxify internal organs like the bowels, liver, kidney, and blood, using natural cleansers. You can apply more specific and advanced techniques such as IV nutrient therapy. There are different detoxification therapies, and they can be applied as needed by the individual on a case-by-case basis.

Although most people can carry out a pure natural cleanse by themselves, it is advised that, just as it is with traditional medicine, the most benefits are reaped when guided by a professional in the field. Working with a healthcare provider or health coach through the detoxification process is a great way to get the maximum benefit from the process. What's more, a health coach can liaise with your medical doctor to help manage all other treatments so that your health continues to improve.

A Body in Motion Stays in Motion

Your body was designed to be in motion. When you stop being active or slow down your regular movement, your aging process accelerates.

Physical inactivity—in other words, lack of exercise—is a significant cause of many chronic diseases and is also detrimental to health and wellness.[37] Conversely, physical exercise provides a whole lot of health benefits at relatively low costs.

We view physical exercise as a form of therapy. When compared to other types of treatment, the benefits of physical exercise are rarely surpassed. It is readily available and has almost no adverse side effects. Physical exercise affects the homeostasis of the entire body and influences multiple body systems. For instance, exercise helps to maintain blood flow to the cerebral area. It also increases oxygen supplied to the cardiovascular system. When you exercise, you stimulate the growth of muscle mass as you develop and age, improve embolism and hormonal systems, and prevent chronic diseases such as obesity, diabetes, cardiovascular disease, neurological conditions, and even cancer.[38]

Going back in history, we can see that active lifestyles were a way of life. Hunting, gathering, and farming were required to survive. Today, it isn't necessary to kill, find, or grow your own food. The human race is now more sedentary than at any other time in history. For many, their jobs and daily routines do not require them to exert themselves physically. Thus, they do not get a proper amount of physical activity necessary for good health.

Sitting too much and moving too little can make you more prone to injury than if you have an active lifestyle. If you sit at a desk every day or regularly play video games, you may have suffered the effects of the sedentary lifestyle—such as repetitive stress injuries.

Your body is meant to be physical and active. The best form of exercise from an integrative healthcare point of view is strength training, which builds muscle while adding to your quality of life in a myriad of ways. Strength training (also called *weight training or resistance training*) is designed to improve muscular fitness but also improves physical balance, heart health, bone strength, and weight loss.

Furthermore, adding just one pound of muscle will allow your body to burn an additional 1,500 calories each month. Combining strength training and cardiovascular exercise gives your body the intensity of movement it needs to stay strong and healthy.

The Physical Activity Guidelines for Americans released by the U.S. Department of Health and Human Services recommends children and adolescents between the ages six and seventeen incorporate some strength training into a routine of sixty minutes for up to three days per week. Adults, on the other hand, were advised to do moderate to intense muscle-strengthening workouts that will target all muscle groups for two days a week.

Strength training can be accomplished with or without the use of weights. It decreases stress in your body, helps balance hormones, and reduces the effects of the primary stress hormone, *cortisol*. Cortisol is one of the main hormones involved in your fight-or-flight response, and regular exercise can reduce its production.

There is a right way to exercise so that you can get the maximum benefit in as little as fifteen to forty-five minutes a week. Check out Dr. Charles Webb's book, *Metamorphosis*, and *Body by Science* by Dr. Doug McGuff, for the best, most efficient forms of strength training. Believe it or not, too much exercise can actually cause you to gain weight or make it difficult to lose weight and increase your risk of injury. These resources can help you know the optimum approach for your exercise plan. Technically speaking, you don't get better during the workout itself; it's the time between workouts that actually build muscles. Ideally, you should give yourself a minimum of a day in between workouts.

Physical exercise, especially strength training, is vital for achieving and maintaining optimal health and wellness. Regular exercise has many benefits. It improves your mood and can be an effective antidepressant. You sleep better when you exercise regularly. You may lower your risk for chronic diseases, such as heart disease and diabetes, as well as cancer and strokes. Now you see why you should make regular exercise a part of your whole health foundation.

Social, Emotional, and Spiritual Health

Healthy social, emotional, and spiritual relationships are essential components of integrative health. You are a social being, and you need a healthy level of social involvement to live a full life. Feeling bonded to other people and having a sense of spiritual connection to something greater than yourself creates richness in your human experience that sets the stage for you to thrive.

Your emotional health affects your ability to recognize, accept, and express feelings adequately. It is related to your ability to control your emotions and maintain a realistic outlook on life and life's situation. That also affects your sense of self-esteem. The link between emotions and health is quite clear, exemplified by disorders such as anxiety and depression.

You may periodically experience undue stress in your personal relationships. This could be a sign that your ego is getting in the way. Be mindful of when this happens. You might be creating emotional barriers to your health and wellness without realizing you are.

Spiritual health relates to your sense of purpose, a feeling of being connected to something greater than yourself. Many people find this in a faith or a belief system. A person with a sense of purpose is healthier than someone without.

Nevertheless, you should recognize that spiritual connection does not necessarily mean practicing a religion. Spending time in nature or exercising may spark your affinity with a higher power or promote a sense of oneness with all living things. Pay attention to what moves *your spirit*. This is the core of your spiritual connection.

Your spiritual health affects other areas of your health, too, like emotional and social health. It allows you to retain a proper outlook on life. It relates to social health because your purpose in life is not in isolation. Meeting and connecting with other people who share that belief or purpose helps you feel accepted and loved, which promotes health and well-being in all other areas of your health as well.

Nutrition and Supplementation

What you eat is the bedrock of your health and wellness. It is a famous saying that we are what we eat.

You must be able to answer the question: Are you eating for your optimal health?

Not all *healthy* foods are healthy for *your body*. What do I mean by that?

Because of today's methods for growing and processing foods, you could be one of the many people suffering from food allergies or sensitivities. Livescience says, "70 percent of Americans surveyed who avoided gluten did so because of celiac disease. In all other countries surveyed, higher percentages of people avoided gluten due to the disease and lower percentages avoided the protein due to gluten sensitivity, the researchers found."[39] Dairy, sugar, and artificial sweeteners are now commonly known among health experts to be quite inflammatory to our bodies as well.

According to BreastCancer.org, diet is partially responsible for between 30 and 40 percent of all cancer cases. Overeating protein or eating the wrong types of proteins can cause numerous problems, such as muscle wasting, reduced immunity because of a weak immune system, lack of energy, and liver problems. Your body processes the proteins that you consume to build muscle, form red and white blood cells, and synthesize hormones and enzymes.

How do you know if you have a food allergy or sensitivity? Start by noticing how you feel:

Do you feel bloated after you eat?

Do you have frequent stomach pain or digestive issues?

If you are noticing problems that you suspect are nutrition-related, keep a food journal for a few days and note what you eat and how you feel. Then enlist the help of experts. Ask your functional medicine doctor to do a comprehensive blood test to help uncover the root of the problem. Talk with your doctor, health coach, or nutritionist about a food elimination diet to help you determine what foods could be sabotaging your health.

If you continue to eat the foods that irritate your digestive system, the result will be tragic. You will be susceptible to inflammation and quickly compromise your health. That puts you at risk for chronic diseases. The key is to identify food allergies and sensitivities as soon as possible and adjust your diet right away. Not only will this relieve your symptoms, but it can possibly stop long-term health issues in their tracks.

Eating only the right food for your body isn't merely for the good of your tummy.

If you find that you are intolerant to certain foods and eliminate them from your diet, you will likely experience other benefits to your whole health, such as:

1. Dramatic improvements in your mood

2. Sharper cognitive abilities

3. Increased energy

Once the problem foods are identified, your functional-medicine doctor, health coach, or nutritionist can help you create a new diet that's appropriate for you. They will help you replace the *bad* foods with good ones and make sure you continue to eat a balanced, healthy diet that supports your optimal health.

Information abounds everywhere on what to eat and what not to eat. Almost every food and supplement is marketed as being safe and even advantageous to your system.

Of course, while the statements are not exactly lying, there is a great deal of misinterpretation and deception. If you follow marketing messages, you will run into trouble. You should research almost everything you eat; you are the number one party to your health, and you should ensure that you pay close attention to everything that enters your mouth. Going further, work with your nutritionist, doctor, or integrative health coach to determine what is best for you.

If you're eating healthy food that's good for your body, do you still need to take supplements?

The answer is *yes*—even if you're eating from the Garden of Eden.

Unfortunately, the proliferation of genetically modified food has depleted nutrients from the soil and the foods that are grown in it. The result is, no matter how healthfully you eat; your diet alone doesn't supply your body with adequate nutrition.

Stress is an additional factor. When you live with constant daily stress, your body quickly metabolizes food to help it mitigate the effects of stress. This can limit the quantity of nutrients your body has time to absorb, creating vitamin and mineral deficiencies. You should see a licensed healthcare provider who has specialized training in proper supplementation to help you determine your body's nutritional and supplementation needs.

If you're wondering where to start with supplements, my recommendation is that, at the very least, you take a high-quality multivitamin, a separate vitamin D3, fish oil, and a good probiotic. It is best to get pharmaceutical-grade supplements that are sold almost exclusively through a licensed healthcare provider.

Although the prices are tempting, beware of supplements sold in the bigger retail chains as recent studies and exposés have shown that most *off the shelf* vitamins and supplements sold do not contain the active ingredients.[40] It's also best not to buy supplements that are resold through retail sites such as Amazon because they may be stored in non-climate-controlled warehouses for extended periods before they are sold and shipped to the customer. Extreme temperatures can compromise the chemical composition and integrity of the active ingredients.

I have one last comment about supplementation. Although yogurt contains some live cultures, eating it will not give you the proper amount or types of probiotics your gut needs to create a balanced bacterial environment. For those of you who are intolerant to dairy products, eating yogurt may actually cause you more harm than good.

Your Hormones Must Be Balanced

The human body is an evolutionary wonder. The sheer complexity that goes into seemingly normal processes is mind-blowing. Have you ever wondered, though, how it all gets controlled? The answer is hormones. Every part of your body, from your brain to your skin, muscles, heart, and kidneys, has a specific job. The endocrine system directs them to carry out each of their duties. The endocrine system is a system of glands that send out hormones: complex chemicals that tell your body what to do, how to do it, and how long to do it.

They are the chemical messengers of the body, traveling through your blood to various tissues and organs to assist in doing the work required of them. They work relatively slowly and affect a high number of processes, such as metabolism, growth, sexual, and reproductive functions.

It might interest you to know that your body produces over 600 different types of hormones. Can you imagine what happens when your hormones are out of balance?

Besides the major female and male reproductive hormones—estrogen, testosterone, and progesterone—other hormones can wreak havoc on your mind and body if they are out of balance. They are your stress-related hormones—cortisol and DHEA—and your thyroid hormones—TSH, T4, and T3.

How do hormone imbalances impact your health?

If, for example, your body does not produce enough of the thyroid hormone T3 or Free T3, you can take a synthetic hormone replacement until you're blue in the face—but you still won't be healthy if your gut and liver don't function properly. Gastrointestinal and liver functions are necessary to convert T4. Thyroid medicines trigger your body to convert T4 into T3, the more active of the thyroid hormones. This again underscores the need to regularly detoxify your body so that the pathways that convert T4 into T3 are clean enough to do their jobs. Further, you need to have a balanced bacterial environment in your gut—by supplementing with a good probiotic—so that your body can absorb the hormones your body or thyroid medication is producing.

See how the systems in your body depend on one another?

Like food allergies and sensitivities, hormone imbalances can result from eating genetically modified foods. Soy is a great example. Soy contains phytoestrogens called *isoflavones* that can hinder the function of your body's natural estrogen and cause hormonal imbalances.

What about cortisol?

Cortisol is the primary stress hormone that regulates your fight-or-flight response. If you are chronically stressed, your body may produce more cortisol than it needs. High levels of cortisol can lead to adrenal fatigue, depression, anxiety, back pain, insomnia, and weight gain, among other disorders. Healthy nutrition, along with exercise and other stress-reduction techniques, can help you keep the effects of chronic stress and your cortisol levels in check.

By no means is this information intended to be a textbook lesson in hormone function, biology, or physiology. It is simply intended to draw your attention to the need for your body to be in balance. Your hormones need to work in concert with one another. If they are unbalanced, even for short periods, the environment will be right for your health to break down. You must prioritize working with a licensed health expert who specializes in understanding and reversing hormone imbalances.

The Integrative Medicine Model

Imagine a circle, and at the center of that circle is Da Vinci's *Vitruvian Man.* Surrounding the outer edges of that circle are the modalities that are included in an ideal integrative healthcare model:

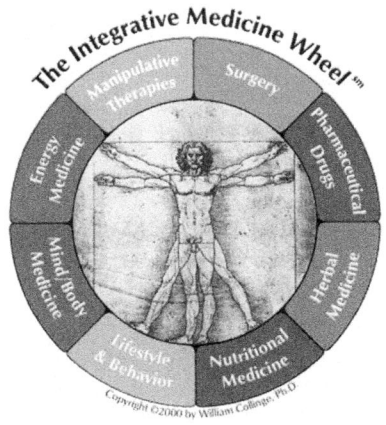

- Medically necessary surgery

- Medically necessary pharmaceutical drugs, when the benefits are scientifically proven to outweigh the side effects

- Herbal medicine

- Nutritional medicine

- Lifestyle and behavior strategies, including stress management

- Mind and body medicine

- Energy medicine, such as qigong and Reiki

- Manipulation therapies, such as traditional chiropractic treatment

The integrative medicine model encompasses all these components, used together or individually, to meet the unique needs of the individual patient.

CHAPTER 3

IS ALTERNATIVE MEDICINE REALLY YOUR BEST ALTERNATIVE?

If you do a quick google search on alternative medicine and its effectiveness, you will almost immediately get discouraged. In fact, the entry on Wikipedia for Alternative Medicine has a tone so negative that it would have you believe that it is all about a bunch of quacks looking to make a quick buck by exploiting others.

That you have read this book up to this point means you should know by now that is not the whole story. Let's take a closer look at alternative medicine on its own and in conjunction with what is known as complementary medicine.

WHAT IS ALTERNATIVE MEDICINE?

Alternative medicine is, broadly speaking, any form of treatment used instead of standard treatments. While this definition seems quite vague, it is accepted because the forms that make up alternative medicine span a wide range of treatment types and classes.

Strictly speaking, standard treatments are based on the results of scientific research and are widely accepted and used. Alternative medicine, however, has lesser research, at least for many of those treatments. The treatments are more primitive in nature, usually passed down from one generation to another, and depend on the practitioner's skill. As a general rule, these treatments are less standardized in terms of application and often rely on the practitioner's intuition and experience rather than a set of rules, as you'd see in allopathic medicine.

Alternative medicine treatments can take many forms, such as special diets, particular types of teas, vitamin supplements, herbal preparations, and cures.

If It's Not Effective, Why Are Many People Still Using It?

First off, if alternative medicine is not as effective as it claims to be, why are more people embracing it? For example, as far back as 2012, Americans spent over $30 billion on alternative medicine.[41] In Canada, people spent $5.6 billion out of their own pockets for alternative care, not backed by insurance, which was paltry when compared to the $31.1 billion spent on conventional medicine and pharmaceutical drugs. But the exciting factor is the rate at which more people are turning to older and more alternative methods of treatment.

We have established that in our modern-day world, more people are getting sicker, and one would expect that more people should be turning to well-known and conventional methods of treatments. But as was discussed in the first chapter, it very often makes matters worse. We are trying to treat problems caused by unhealthy lifestyles and the consumption of unnatural and engineered substances such as GMOs and other artificial chemicals, with more artificial chemicals in the form of prescription drugs. Little wonder, then, that these treatments are ineffective and often cause more harm.

It stands to reason then that many people begin to search for alternative means of treatment after seeing the harm caused to their loved ones and people around them. What is most interesting to me, however, is how, with the overwhelming pressure by the media—sponsored by Big Pharma, of course— more people are turning to alternative forms of treatment. That means that despite how loudly the media is promoting traditional allopathic medicine and trying to discredit alternative and complementary forms of treatment, more people are discovering that something is not right and are taking steps necessary to change it.

For example, Deb Matthews, the Minister for Health and Long-Term Care in Ontario, was quoted as saying in 2011 that Traditional Chinese Medicine, a form of alternative therapy, played a valuable role in the health and welfare of many Ontarians. More people were choosing complementary and alternative approaches to healthcare.[42]

In my clinical experience, it was rare to hear of patients requiring long-term care for chronic illnesses or diseases seeking alternative solutions. Now, however, it is repeatedly spoken of. People want their health restored. They are tired of all the side effects from drug therapy. They have family and friends who are worn out from hospital stays and surgeries. They are broken—physically, financially, and emotionally. People today are seeking restorative, life-altering, alternative solutions for themselves and their loved ones. They are also realizing that an optimistic perspective greatly enhances their chances for not only survival, but truly rewarding outcomes. Once upon a time, going to a psychologist was seen as a negative; patients today are realizing that mental health is a primary step in the right direction.

I'd say the awareness people now have toward the decisions they are making, along with their newfound purpose to govern their own affairs, especially after having watched their parents die so grievously—while faithfully taking all their prescribed drugs or seeing the horrible side-effects all the immunizations have had on their children—is truly sparking something remarkable in our societies today.

This interest in a healthier way of life has also spurred some governments to attempt to regulate the sector, and, in a fashion typical of their usual disdain for alternative treatments, they like to say that alternative medicine has minimal scientific validity.

Do healthcare providers believe that making recommendations for alternative treatments to patients is unethical? Well, for some, that may absolutely be the case.

Let me first say, however, that I know for a fact there are many good medical practitioners who truly desire to help their patients. Their hearts break when they cannot help them. They get just as frustrated as you do when things don't go well. Most of them are on the good side, but traditional medical practice, as a whole, leaves much to be desired.

Not only is it taxing us financially, but also physically and mentally. It has already been established that medical science cannot say they have a cure for anything. They have drugs that mask the symptoms, generally while silently, and sometimes irreparably, creating new ones.

Some surgeries have left people disfigured, disabled, disoriented, and seeking psychological help to unravel a new hell they have been thrown into. Their bodies have been mutilated, their thinking distorted, and their bank accounts emptied.

So where do we go from here? I realize there are charlatans who claim to have the cure for anything and everything that ails you. I also believe that they have been around since the beginning of time.

But I also believe that there are some profoundly effective remedies for the things that plague us.

The bad news? As in anything in life, if someone can't make money off it, they generally don't want to share. It has always been about the buck, not just in medicine, but in all aspects of life.

The good news? Reliable information is available—thankfully we still have the web to help us find things we are searching for. Hopefully we have a great support system of friends and family to help us as well.

The main thing to remember is that *you*, the patient, are in charge of your life and the care you receive.

Do people ever get better using traditional medical practices? Absolutely! Sometimes, drugs and surgeries are the only viable solution.

But could there also be a better way for some of the things we have been used to doing? A different way perhaps? The ancient paths may be just the thing that we should be seeking.

First step? Ask your general practitioner if they can help you find an alternative solution. You may be surprised. If for some reason they say they cannot help you, then by all means, go find someone who can, or start your own search. The most miraculous stories of healing have almost always been the ones where people start digging because they aren't satisfied with the status quo and refuse to give up, or give in.

With respect to the individual experience, we should be aware of not only the organic sphere of illness and disease, but of the practical effects of the healing modality and experience, as well.

Be persistent! Be bold! Be proactive! *Be alive!*

Classification of Alternative Medicine

Alternative medicine treatments are numerous, as they are drawn from many cultures, schools of thought, and periods in history. As we have seen, historical lifestyles were generally healthier than our current lifestyles, and as such, it is essential to reflect on history to understand their techniques and adapt them to help the sick in our world today. Alternative Medicine can generally be classified into five major categories:

- **Alternative medical systems**: These are healing and healthcare systems from other cultures, which include acupuncture, herbal medicine, homeopathy, and spiritual healing.

- **Mind-body techniques**: These have to do with treatments that affect the mind, soul, and emotions as much, if not more than, the body. They include hypnotherapy, art therapy, music therapy, meditation, prayer therapy, dance therapy, guided imagery, and yoga.

- **Biologically based therapies**: These therapies improve wellness by using natural products and assisting nature to do its job in our bodies. Therapies such as diets and dietary supplements, herbal products, and multivitamins belong in this category.

- **Energy therapies**: These techniques guide or use some sort of soul or spirit energy to restore and maintain health and wellness. Some of the types are qigong, prana, therapeutic touch, and Reiki.

- **Manipulative and body-based therapies**: These include techniques such as acupressure, the Trager Approach, chiropractic, reflexology, and osteopathy.

What Does the Research Say
About Alternative Medicine?

Ancient systems of health and healing have been around for thousands of years before conventional medicine. Although there is little research to support the success rate of ancient medicine, it obviously worked, since the human species survived, thrived, and evolved. Mainstream conventional physicians may argue that since ancient medicine is still not scientifically proven, it is not viable. Advising patients on decision making with input based on evidence should be the minimum for primary care physicians. But according to a new study in the *British Journal of Medicine*, only 18 percent of clinical recommendations are based on high-quality evidence, which leaves 82 percent of all conventional medical treatments scientifically unproven.[43] Most scientific studies can be broken down into observational (observing something that happens) and experimental (which involve scientists controlling some of the variables). Generally, experimental studies are considered to provide stronger evidence and clearer cause and effect.[44] Further, two recent studies in the New England Journal of Medicine have caused uproar in the research community by finding no difference in estimates of treatment effects between randomized controlled trials and non-randomized trials.[45]

Even so, the traditional medical community seems to be content with what it knows and is resistant to exploring complementary and alternative modalities. That's why it's so crucial for you to share your interest in these health and wellness options with your healthcare provider to encourage an open, curious dialogue that involves you in your own healthcare decisions.

Most conventional medical research is funded by big pharmaceutical companies. It's no coincidence that the same companies funding the research are also promoting their own specific agenda—to design and sell drugs.

Funding for research on the efficacy of complementary and alternative modalities is limited without the support of the pharmaceutical industry. The creation of the National Center for Complementary and Alternative Medicine lends credence to the legitimacy of these treatment modalities and provides funding opportunities for associated research and development.

Do alternative treatment options work?

The short answer is *yes*.

Despite what the media—which is sponsored heavily by large pharmaceuticals looking to sell drugs—would have you think, alternative treatments do work in many situations.

Just like conventional medicine, they work under the right conditions focused on the exact situation. No one treatment option—traditional *or* alternative—is right for every person every time.

Another clue that these treatments work is that more alternative treatments are being covered by health insurance. If your insurance company covers a particular treatment, that should signal you to consider that treatment a legitimate option. Insurance companies do not pay for treatments they deem as illegitimate healthcare options. The list of covered alternative treatments is expanding, a sign that insurance companies are taking them seriously. Take a look at your health insurance policy benefits. Chances are that alternative treatments such as massage, acupuncture, and chiropractic visits are on the list. If you have a health savings plan, you may have used your accrued savings to pay for supplements and nutraceuticals— food-derived supplements. That's progress.

Although some proponents of conventional medicine may assert that alternative treatments are quackery, alternative treatment options are regaining acceptance because of their effectiveness. The perception is coming in full circle—from ancient modalities to conventional medicine to alternative options with roots to ancient patterns. Conventional medicine became necessary because of lifestyle diseases that weren't an issue some generations ago, not because the older modalities didn't work. They just weren't aggressive enough to effectively handle modern illness and acute situations.

What's happening now can be the best of both worlds *if* healthcare providers from all modalities will accept the merits of all options and use them collectively as a whole health approach. The other piece of this puzzle is you, and how involved you choose to be in your healthcare.

Knowing what you know now, it should become evident that you need to be actively involved in your healthcare. You cannot leave your health and your continuous well-being to a doctor. After all, no one can truly understand you and your unique situation more than you do. Blindly perpetuating the myth that the *doctor knows best*, will continue to lend credibility to traditional medicine in all cases even when it may only be most appropriate for acute care.

What Is Complementary and Alternative Medicine?

We can see that both conventional and alternative medicine have distinct advantages over each other, with each style of treatment proffering incredible insight into the human body, as well as providing relief and cure from various illnesses. If both admittedly impressive treatment approaches are combined, we can begin to operate complementary medicine.

According to everydayhealth.com:

> Complementary and alternative medicine, or CAM, is a category of medicine that includes a host of different treatment approaches that generally fall outside the realm of conventional medicine, which includes treatments like drug therapies and surgeries. There is an increasing amount of research being done to establish the safety and efficacy of alternative medicine.[46]

Compared to traditional Western therapies, alternative medicine still has limited research data to back it up due to funding constraints and opposition from large pharmaceuticals and the traditional medical community.

Even though CAM combines complementary and alternative medicine into one category, there is actually a difference between the two. *Complementary medicine* refers to healing practices or products, such as supplements or nutraceuticals, that work in conjunction with traditional medicine. For example, cancer patients who are undergoing chemotherapy may also use acupuncture as a complementary treatment to help manage the chemotherapy side effects. In my current practice as a clinical psychologist and a certified wellness coach, many of my clients use this technique to blend their treatment options. Complementary medicine is not a substitute for traditional therapies; it's an adjunct.

Alternative medicine is different in that it's not used as a complement to, but as a substitute for, traditional therapies or treatments. For example, instead of using chemotherapy and radiation to treat cancer, someone might choose to make specific dietary changes.

More Americans are using alternative treatment modalities. More than 40 percent of adults and 12 percent of children are using some form of alternative therapies. In my clinical experience, women with higher education and incomes, ages forty to sixty, are the most frequent users of complementary and alternative therapies.

In fact, there are specific categories of complementary and alternative medicine. There is *mind-body medicine*, which focuses on how your mental and emotional status relates to and affects your body's ability to function. Examples of this are meditation and art therapy. Mind-body therapy refers to a complete system of medical theory and practice that goes back thousands of years and includes traditional Chinese medicine and Ayurvedic medicine, which originated in India. Western whole medical systems include homeopathy and naturopathy.

Another category of complementary and alternative medicine includes manipulation and body-based practices, which rely on physical manipulation of the body to improve specific symptoms and overall health, such as chiropractic and osteopathy.

Energy medicine is yet another category that uses the body and spirit energy fields to promote healing. *Biofield therapies* affect energy fields, which are said to encircle the body, such as auras or chakras. Forms of energy medicine include Reiki, qigong, and magnet therapy. Then there are biologically based practices that focus on herbs, nutrition, vitamins, and dietary supplements. Herbal medicines are the most common form of biologically based complementary and alternative medicine.

WARNING! If you are considering using complementary or alternative therapies, make sure you consult with a primary care provider who is familiar with complementary and alternative therapies. Do some research on your own as well. If you are taking any kind of prescription medicine, make sure you work with your doctor first to determine if you should continue taking your medications or if it's safe to discontinue them. Sometimes combining the two can have catastrophic results.

When you speak with your physician, make sure he or she is educated about the specific complementary or alternative modalities you're inquiring about. Do your research first so that you can help your physician understand what you hope to accomplish. The Institute for Functional Medicine website at IFM.org is a trusted resource for reliable information that you can use and to which you can refer your practitioner for an understanding of complementary and alternative treatments.

Frankenfoods and Attitudes

Beware of Frankenfoods—as discussed in the first chapter, these are foods genetically engineered with plant or animal components—because they affect not only your attitudes, but also your body. I use this term to describe anything food related that is created in a lab, like all processed foods. What you don't know about your diet can hurt you, and if you don't know what the ingredient is, you shouldn't eat it.

Frankenfoods have been linked to the proliferation of today's lifestyle diseases—heart disease, diabetes, cancer, and autoimmune disorders. They also negatively affect your mood and cognitive functioning, and can directly cause depression, anxiety, brain fog, a sense of general malaise, and irritability, and can exacerbate food sensitivities and allergies.

Many experts believe that the dramatic increase in autism rates is a direct result of the mothers' digestive issues before birth, likely caused by Frankenfoods.

Your body was simply not designed to metabolize processed and synthetic foods. Although it can adapt for a while, if you continue to eat fake food, your gut will eventually break down.

Furthermore, research shows that Frankenfoods lead to nutritional deficiencies. Many new clients come to my practice with dietary deficiencies. They are malnourished. If you are eating Frankenfoods, and not getting the proper nutrients your body needs to be healthy, you will be malnourished. Malnutrition is not a problem confined only to underdeveloped countries. As discussed earlier, even if you're eating from the Garden of Eden, you will need to add high-quality nutritional supplements to your diet to achieve optimum nutrition and whole health.

You can't live a balanced life in body, mind, and spirit and feel optimal health and wellness if you are malnourished. Pay attention to what you eat. Make it a point to stay away from Frankenfoods and feed your body the best quality foods right for you. You will set yourself up to feel, and be, healthy.

Is Alternative Healthcare Affordable?

Unequivocally, the answer is *yes*.

You will always find the resources for the things that are most important to you. Whether it's a new car, new twenty-inch wheels for your car, or going to yoga class, you'll find a way to make it happen if you want it.

Is good health important to you?

You should consider your good health as the most important investment you can make in your life, one that will pay you big dividends. If you're not well and you're not getting better, continuing to spend money on treatments that aren't working for you becomes an expense—not an investment—in your health.

Find a physician who specializes in functional medicine and has expertise in diagnosing and treating the underlying cause of your illness. Unless you manage the cause of your disease, you will only mask the symptoms. Treating symptoms does not lead to sustainable improvements in your health, and it only results in increased expenses rather than long-term beneficial investments.

Complementary and alternative modalities are affordable. Many insurance companies will now cover these services too. More stores are carrying a wide variety of organic products at more affordable prices. As the demand for high-quality foods rises, retailers compete more aggressively for your business. Prices for services, such as yoga sessions, are also priced more competitively the more popular they become.

If you want it, you can find it at a price you can afford.

How can you not afford it if you're committed to investing in your good health?

CASE STUDIES

So that you can understand the practical implications and applications of complementary and alternative treatments, I've assembled some case studies to lend credence to the general information presented in this book. My aim is to give you a sense of hope, empowerment, and knowledge about the mechanics and effectiveness of these options.

As you review the case studies, keep in mind that there are only two types of illnesses:

1. Acute illness or infection, such as a broken arm or meningitis

2. Immune system breakdown

If your problem is not an acute situation, it is a breakdown in your immune system. The key is to understand where the failure in your immune system exists and then determine the most appropriate treatment options to address the whole system in a holistic, integrative way. Reviewing the case studies and understanding the two types of illnesses will put you in a better position to make sense of your health and create a lifestyle of wellness for the rest of your life.

Cancer

Please remember that I am not a physician, nor am I claiming to be an expert in the diagnosis or treatment of cancer. See your licensed healthcare provider immediately if you think you may have cancer or if you have other questions about your specific health or medical condition.

Cancer used to seem like some strange, severe illness that happened to other people—people you didn't know. Now it's safe to say that everyone knows someone who has personally experienced or been touched by cancer; I do too. Dr. Bernard Jensen had a remarkable cancer survival story, "Death-Bed Cancer to Cancer Free in Sixty Days," which I'm excited to share with you.[47]

Dr. Jensen was a well-known alternative health practitioner and chiropractor, entrepreneur, and the author of numerous books and articles on health and healing. Even though he had written many books on nutrition and digestive health, years of travel, restaurant food, and lack of good sleep caught up with him; he was literally wasting away due to prostate cancer. He was down to seventy-six pounds. The cancer had metastasized in his bones. At this point, Dr. Jensen's prostate-specific antigen, or PSA, registered well over 1600, where a normal count should be one to four. He was put on unlimited amounts of morphine for pain.

Dr. Jensen had taken residence in Hawaii's Queen's Medical Center, where he was told he was going to die. His traditional medical doctors had written him off. Friends and colleagues said goodbye. In desperation, his wife contacted Dr. Michael O'Brien, a conventional medical practitioner himself, and an old friend of Dr. Jensen's, who ran medical clinics in Los Angeles and was a nutrition formulator.

Dr. O'Brien spoke with Dr. Jensen on his deathbed. After hearing his friend confess that he just wanted to die, Dr. O'Brien challenged Dr. Jensen to show the world that even in his state of decline, it was possible to beat cancer using natural methods. Dr. Jensen accepted the challenge.

Dr. O'Brien knew that he could have a dramatic impact on Dr. Jensen's health, if not reversing cancer, at least cleaning and feeding his body properly. He started with cleaning his bowels, which had been blocked for fifteen days. Days of enemas finally succeeded in normal bowel movements. Then, Dr. O'Brien was convinced that there were only two things Dr. Jensen's body needed to clean itself of the cancer—enzymes and probiotics.

Dr. Jensen's wife gave him massive doses of probiotics and digestive enzymes. Here is an excerpt from his book, Come *Alive!*

On week two, Dr. O'Brien put a pillow behind Dr. Jensen's back so he could sit up and drink water without a straw.

At week three, Dr. Jensen was conducting business over the phone and wrote a letter to Dr. O'Brien telling him how good it felt to be able to take a shower again.

At week four, Dr. Jensen walked to the door to greet Dr. O'Brien when he flew in. He wanted to show Michael how well he was doing.

Week five came along, and Michael and Bernard went out for a ride in the country to look at eagles. Michael knew this would cheer up Bernard.

At week six, Michael took Bernard out for dinner.

Week seven arrived, but Dr. O'Brien couldn't fly in because he had other obligations, so when they got together on week eight, Bernard took Michael hiking. And Bernard had no sign of prostate cancer at all. In fact, Bernard was out-hiking Michael, joking that they needed to turn back, or Bernard may have to carry him back.[48]

Dr. Jensen experienced a remarkable recovery in eight weeks on high doses of nutraceuticals, cleaning and feeding his body, and exercise. They fed his body with probiotics, cleaned out deadly cancer with digestive enzymes, and, as soon as he had the strength, added movement to his treatment plan. Dr. Jensen was one of the foremost experts on colon health, nutrition, and detoxification. It is truly a testimony to his life's work that its tenets were at the core of his healing.

Autoimmune Conditions

More people around the globe are being diagnosed with autoimmune disorders. For a long time, the *autoimmune disorder* was the catchall description of any disease that conventional medical practitioners couldn't pinpoint. Many of my patients were dismissed from traditional healthcare providers who said everything they were feeling was all in their heads. There is more research being conducted on the immune system now, however.

The second case I will give you happened to a very dear friend of mine who was diagnosed with chronic fatigue syndrome about ten years ago. She made her rounds with traditional medical doctors: countless internal medicine doctors, multiple endocrinologists, and a fair share of alternative therapies. They led only to frustration with all the options offered to her.

Finally, she landed with a functional and integrative physician in tandem with a doctor of chiropractic. The integrative chiropractic physician in our clinic also practices Chinese medicine and acupuncture with her. Together they are reversing her thyroid and autoimmune disorder.

My best friend has used the pure gum spirits of turpentine for the past twelve weeks to detox her body. She has also adopted a cleaner, plant-based diet and taken a functional and integrative medicine approach to her health. Finally, she feels relief from her chronic fatigue.

WARNING! Do not attempt to use turpentine therapy without seeking the proper consultation and treatment from your licensed physician. Work with someone who knows what they're doing when considering this as a treatment option.

Mental Health

As an integrative clinical psychologist, I see numerous mental and behavioral health issues with my patients. I always take an integrative approach and regularly recommend prayer, meditation, yoga, Pilates, acupuncture, functional medicine, allergy testing and treatment, chiropractic, Chinese medicine, massage, Reiki, and other whole health approaches.

I recommend body-based interventions because what may at first appear to be a mental health issue is often the symptom of another underlying physical health issue. Many times, the issue is as simple as environmental or food allergies or sensitivities.

Sometimes the problem is caused by hormonal imbalances, a hyperactive or underactive thyroid, or the body overproducing the stress hormone, cortisol.

You are more than a set of symptoms. To help you on the pathway to whole health, it is critical that your healthcare provider identifies the underlying root cause of your problem and does not merely treat your symptoms. If your healthcare provider does not take a whole health approach, there is a high risk of misdiagnosis. If the diagnosis is incorrect, the treatment approach will likely be wrong as well.

Research shows that an integrative approach to health and healing—addressing body, mind, and spirit—is the one approach that allows for the fastest and fullest resolution of symptoms and causes. You are a whole person. An integrative approach honors this by taking your overall functioning—your physical body, relationships, lifestyle habits and behaviors, sleep patterns, stress management, and thinking habits—into account. You can't live fully and experience a life of health and happiness if you do not address all areas of your life.

Finally, I went through a situation myself two summers ago when I suddenly experienced the onset of a severe panic attack while driving. I am self-aware, so I knew I wasn't under any apparent stress. When I examined my whole situation, I realized that I had pushed myself for years, working twelve- to fourteen-hour days, and had not entirely focused on an overall healthy lifestyle. The panic attacks made it clear to me that my body was breaking down, and I needed to make some changes.

Working with one of the doctors in our practice who specializes in functional medicine, I learned my adrenal glands were fatigued. The doctor took a holistic evaluation of my lifestyle to determine the root cause of my adrenal fatigue. The lab results were evaluated based on the ranges of functional medicine rather than the traditional range that most doctors rely on.

Then, the doctor and I discussed my lifestyle, including my work hours, social relationships, and how I managed stress. She suggested a whole health approach to treat my adrenal fatigue, which was triggered by anxiety.

The doctor prescribed vitamin D and rest. Together we crafted a new, reasonable work schedule. We fortified my diet by increasing my daily intake of fresh vegetables and water and eliminating coffee. This whole health approach was explicitly designed to rebuild my adrenal function and stop my overproduction of cortisol, which kept me in fight-or-flight mode. I soon felt better, and the panic attacks stopped.

Mental health is not always purely a mental health issue. That's why it's vital to take an integrative approach and evaluate your situation holistically. Be open to exploring all your options.

Know that big success can come from small changes. Remember to be patient with yourself. The right combination of treatments for your whole health will heal your body and mind inside out. You might not see dramatic changes immediately but give it time and love yourself through the process.

IS ALTERNATIVE MEDICINE THE RIGHT APPROACH FOR EVERY BODY?

The answer is yes . . . and no.

Your approach to healthcare should be as unique and individual as you and your situation are.

At Dr. Aimee & Associates and The Center for Integrative and Functional Health and Wellness, your treatment begins with a careful and comprehensive initial evaluation to gain an understanding of your health issues and lifestyle—the keys to your whole long-term health. We want to know what's going on in your life so that we can get to the root cause of your health issues.

We want to know:

- Do you have stable relationships?

- What is your work life like?

- What concerns do you have about your health?

- Can you describe your family's health history?

- How do you like to relax?

- What do you do for pleasure and enjoyment?

Understanding how you walk through your life provides clues to how you need to manage your health. Alternative medicine may work correctly for you and your situation but may not work at all for someone else.

The same holds true for any treatment approach. You must also include the common-sense factor. If you have a broken arm, an acute situation, then changing your diet alone is not the most expedient or effective means of treatment, although it could help your healing process. If you have an infection that has been resistant to other forms of intervention, you may want to consider taking an antibiotic.

Alternative medicine isn't the right approach for everybody all the time. Your treatment needs to be carefully discussed with all your health and wellness providers. Then you can make a fully informed decision.

Does It Work?

From my clinical and personal experience, it does work. Again, I know there are many critics of alternative and complementary approaches who say it doesn't work. Their sentiment tends to come from the far-right-wing conventional political mindsets. There is a reason that roughly 40 percent of Americans are now turning to alternative and complementary modalities.[49] The society we live in is getting more informed and savvier in terms of taking control of their health. They are researching more and more. People are not going to continue to spend their hard-earned money—trillions of dollars every year—on treatments that just don't work.

Again, insurance coverage often is available for many of these modalities. It does work. And if you're paying out of pocket and you get your health and your life back, isn't that investment worth it?

Explore with your provider and your health coach to determine what will work for you. What works or does not work is based on many different factors. For instance, you need to take a thorough look at your health history and lifestyle habits.

In most cases, if you ask people who practice yoga if it helps them with stress reduction, they will say yes. If you ask people who have used acupuncture if it helps with pain relief, they will say yes. If you ask people who have experienced Reiki if it brings a sense of peace and calm, they will say yes, it does. If you ask people who do regular bodywork, such as chiropractic adjustments or massage, if it helps them feel better, they will say yes.

Whether it's evidence-based or placebo-based, it really doesn't matter as long as the individual feels there is a benefit. If they are feeling the benefit, their mood will be enhanced, and their immune functioning will be improved because they become more relaxed. When they are more comfortable, when they are in a better mood, their cognitive functioning is enhanced. In my clinical opinion, it absolutely works. In anecdotal vignettes, it absolutely works.

The Role of Food and Nutrition Revisited

You read earlier that Hippocrates was the father of modern medicine. He said, "Let food be your medicine and let your medicine be food." One of the thoughts expressed by the Hippocratic oath is: *Practice two things in your dealings with a disease, either help or do not harm the patient.* This translation is believed to have originated from a nineteenth-century surgeon, Thomas Inman.

Many of the biologically based alternative healthcare systems emphasize the role of food and nutrition in whole health. Keep this in mind if you're tempted to reach for a box of Frankenfood. Frankenfoods harm your body. Real, organic, plant-based, whole foods nourish and heal your body from the inside out.

Did you know that too much acidity has been linked to inflammation, heart disease, obesity, and diabetes?[50]

Understand that I am not a physician, nor am I an expert in diagnosing or treating cancer.

But this statement makes a case for antioxidant foods, which naturally promote alkalinity in your body. Focus on nutritionally robust foods. These tend to be brightly colored foods by nature: eat foods that cover the spectrum of colors in the rainbow.

In addition to eating the rainbow, remember to include supplements that will enrich your body with macro- and micronutrients. These essential nutrients are not found in today's growing environments. With so much of today's foods being processed and genetically modified, it's difficult to get healthy amounts of macro- and micro-nutrients from food alone.

Giving your body the right food and nutrition—a biological treatment system—can successfully reverse most lifestyle-caused diseases while dramatically impacting your mental and behavioral health.

A Revolution in Health and Wellness

The world is facing a revolution in health and wellness. This is more than merely reversing diseases or curing infections. It is about experiencing fulfillment and satisfaction in your life, which can only happen with a healthy mind and a healthy body.

Awareness of whole health—both self-awareness and public awareness—is at a tipping point, and the movement is building. Health and wellness issues are regularly featured in the media, and the benefits of proper nutrition, various movement modalities, and the positive impacts of the whole health approach are frequent topics.

Today it is widely recognized that your health is at the center of everything in your life:

- The success of your relationships

- Your earning ability

- The quality of your sleep

- Your problem-solving abilities

- The kind of parent you are

- How effective and productive you are at work

The healthcare revolution sounded a much-needed alarm on the traditional health models that *it's time to wake up and take notice* of other options that could help patients be healthier. A prime example of this open-minded approach among traditional healthcare providers is Dr. Oz, who is known to have used Reiki with his cardiology patients. This kind of attitude is prevailing and is the start of something special in reclaiming control of your health and your life.

Again, I want to emphasize the importance of working directly with your healthcare provider to determine the best options available for you and your situation. Although the information in this book reflects my personal and professional education, training, beliefs, opinions, and experience, it should not be construed as any kind of professional or medical advice.

CHAPTER 4

HEALTH AND HAPPINESS ARE TEAM SPORTS

THE TEAM APPROACH

To live fully and healthfully, to live a life of happiness and vitality, you must take a team approach to your life. By team, I am not just talking about people in your life or the providers in your life. I am explicitly referring to the three main team members: your body, your mind, and your spirit. You cannot live fully if one or more of those areas are out of balance.

You can have a great body. It can be ripped and beautiful, worthy of the best bodybuilding competition, but if you are struggling with stress or anxiety or even a bad attitude, you can't live fully. Similarly, if you are only focused on your spiritual health and are neglecting your mind, not feeding it with information to help you thrive, or not relating to people who are supportive in your life, you cannot live fully.

You can have a connection with a higher source if that is what is important to you, but if you don't take care of your body, you still won't be living fully. It is essential to employ a holistic and integrative approach to live a full, healthy, satisfying life; hence, the team approach.

Body

Relative to taking care of your body, we have discussed the pillars of health. They include detoxifying your body regularly, understanding the relationship of health and nutrition, ensuring a healthy hormonal balance, and engaging in physical activity. If you have had physical health issues in the past, I would recommend that you develop a working relationship with an excellent integrative, holistic provider and address these factors in this order.

Detox first. You need to have a clean body to absorb nutrition.

Next, focus on your diet: fresh, healthy, plant-based foods. If you are not eating and nourishing your body well, then your hormones will likely be out of balance.

Physical activity should be the last pillar you focus on. Your body was designed to be in motion, not to be sedentary. You must take care of your body. Where exercise and nutrition are concerned, if you are ever in a position where you need to choose between whether to focus on diet *or* exercise—for instance, if you are short on time and can either prepare a healthy meal or take the time to exercise, always choose food first.

In terms of what kind of exercise is best, most experts will tell you that strength training is by far the most beneficial to your mind and your body. Strength training allows you to have healthy joints and bones, and it will enable you to have a good quality of life. Cardiovascular health is good but having a robust and healthy heart does not mean you will live long or have a higher quality of life. I know lots of runners who have heart disease. The ideal form of exercise is strength training.

Rest is of utmost importance. It is crucial to have good sleep hygiene. Every hour of sleep that you get before midnight is worth two hours of sleep in terms of the quality of your sleep. "Just 15 minutes of meditation each day helps to bring a balance to an otherwise overwhelmed life. It gives us back a little of what we lose when we don't get enough sleep, helps us to focus, heal, and cope."[51]

Part of having a healthy body means taking time to sleep. Ideally, for most adults, that means getting at least seven and a half to eight hours of sleep each night. Precisely the amount of sleep your body needs may vary, but seven and a half to eight hours of sleep is ideal for most adults. Children and adolescents generally need more sleep because growth occurs during sleep. Proper rest is essential to having a healthy body.

Mind

Your mind was designed to be on purpose. What I mean by that is that it was intended to be a goal-achieving machine. To fully activate your mind's function, you must have some sort of intellectual stimulation. A brilliant mind that does not have a sense of purpose or direction is a mess.

I'm sure you can think of someone you know who has a high IQ but doesn't have a sense of purpose or direction in their life. They are almost always stressed, unhappy, or having trouble finding meaning.

Our minds were designed to help us evolve. Even though we don't always have the same goals—nor should we—we will essentially flounder our way through life if we live without goals or a sense of direction. A life without purpose and design is chaotic. Our minds were designed to be stimulated and to work purposefully toward something meaningful. Whatever is meaningful is specific to individuals.

To live fully in mind, body, and spirit, you must have some sort of purpose or direction for your life. A mind without a purpose or course is like a ship without a rudder. It's either going to sink or run aground. Your mind was designed to be continuously moving toward something—a goal, a dream, a desire.

When you set a goal or make up your mind to do something, it's as though magic happens. Your conscious mind and your subconscious mind work in alignment to influence your thoughts and your feelings. This has the effect of changing your behaviors, which subsequently allow you to achieve the goal you set out to accomplish.

Your mind works best when you are looking forward to something or when you are stimulated. For example, children are happiest in anticipation of Christmas, even before the gifts are opened. How about the excitement one experiences in looking forward to a vacation?

Indeed, these are simple examples, but they are meant to demonstrate that we are happiest when our minds are engaged and looking forward to, or working toward, a goal. That's how we have evolved, and we will continue to develop, by engaging our minds in meaningful tasks and pursuits.

Spiritual Health

To live fully, you must entirely join your body, mind, and spirit. Whether you believe in God, the divine, the universe, source of energy, or a higher power, it's crucial to be connected to something greater than yourself. You can nourish your soul by staying connected to whatever it is that is meaningful to you. It could be prayer or connecting in nature. A wise person once said, "We came from somewhere, so we must be going somewhere."

A simple way to feed your spiritual self is to find meaning in things or experiences. For some, it could be reconnecting to a religion. For others, it could be finding a sense of peace or centeredness from spending time outdoors in nature. Meditating and listening to music that lifts your spirit are other ways to feed your spiritual self.

Another part of minding your spiritual health involves listening to your wiser self or your intuition. Sometimes, it is referred to as your *higher self.* You can do this by getting quiet and asking your wise self for guidance on simple decisions.

Learn to trust your instincts. Part of connecting to your spiritual self is trusting your instincts. Your instincts come from this part of yourself that is connected to God and source. It's interesting to note that when people say *trust your gut instincts*, it's because your gut—literally your gastrointestinal system—has more sensory receptors than any other part of your body.

Your gut sensory receptors are designed to pick up energy. In prehistoric times, that allowed us to determine whether something was safe or unsafe. When people say *trust your instincts*, really—trust your instincts. That is one of the easiest ways to learn to connect to your spiritual or higher self. That is the part of yourself that is all-knowing.

FINANCIAL HEALTH

It's important to focus on your financial health because you can't live a fully satisfying life without enough money. You must invest in your financial health. A lack of financial reserves is the biggest obstacle for my clients—and most people—to living the lives they desire.

In fact, money is often one of the main reasons for divorce.[52] It's not necessarily how much or how little money couples have, it's because people generally think about money differently, and therefore have different money habits. It is essential to have a strong sense of financial health if you want to live a life of happiness and health.

What Is Financial Health and Why Does It Matter?

Remember, we talked about our basic survival needs?

Our most basic needs are food, clothing, and shelter. The greatest fears that people have today are not having enough money, and/or outliving their money in retirement. And who doesn't hope to leave money to someone they love when they pass.[53] If we consider popular survey answers, we may think the greatest fear is the fear of public speaking. But if people are truly being honest, the number one fear is being without enough money. It absolutely matters.

If we lived in a society where the currency was fish, we would need enough fish. But we live in a society where we exchange money, so money is essential.

Financial health is not only directly tied to our survival needs, but also to our physical, mental, and spiritual health. If we worry every day about how to make ends meet, we are not going to be living fully in spirit, or mind, or body for that matter, because that stress is going to undermine our immune system.

Also, our financial health matters in terms of our employability. Believe it or not, more and more employers are checking our credit history. Your insurance company checks your credit rating. If you are going to the bank to get a loan, whether it is for a house, a personal line of credit for your business, or an auto loan, they evaluate your financial *worthiness*. Having a strong sense of financial health matters a lot because it opens a lot more doors and leads the way to more opportunities.

And from a social desirability perspective, people generally want to be partnered with somebody who has healthy financial habits. Again, one of the top causes of divorce is money.

The Role of Money in Emotional, Physical, and Spiritual Health

If we don't have enough money to meet our basic needs, we are going to be preoccupied and anxious, likely even depressed. Physically, anything that causes us to worry sets us up for physical health problems, whether it's sleep disturbance, a lowered immune system, or just being more susceptible to illness.

Excessive and chronic worry undermines our physical health and changes our hormones; it is also likely to cause inflammation. Inflammation is a precursor to many health issues. For example, worrying about your financial health could cause an upset stomach, a headache, or acid reflux. Those are just a few ways that worrying about money causes us to have physical reactions.

Emotionally, if we are preoccupied with how we are going to make ends meet, we are going to be anxious and irritable. Not having enough money is often a significant precursor to depression. Worry makes it hard for us to connect and stay invested in taking care of the other things we need to do. Constantly worrying about how we are going to pay bills will impact our relationships. If we are worrying about money, a typical emotional result is more conflict within our interpersonal relationships.

Similarly, your spiritual health is undermined.

Can you relax and connect to God, nature, or anything else if you are always worried about how you are going to pay your rent?

The constant worry about money affects every aspect of your life.

Whatever you are thinking about affects each area of your life: mentally, emotionally, physically, interpersonally, and spiritually. If you are preoccupied, worrying about money, you won't be able to be as productive at work. You won't be as efficient. Improving your financial health begins with understanding the role money plays in your emotional, physical, and spiritual health.

How to Achieve Financial Health

To achieve financial health, you must invest in changing your mindset and your actions. You will need to do inner and outer work. The inner work consists of making changes in how you think and how you feel about money.

A lot of my coaching clients come to see me to help them understand their money mindset. That's the blueprint, if you will, that was impressed upon us during our early formative years: watching the role models in our lives—our parents, the people we knew and trusted, the stories we heard about money, the beliefs we heard. All these experiences shaped how we view our circumstances and, likely, how we manage it as well.

Doing the inner work requires you to change the way you think and feel about money. That means identifying and changing your beliefs about money and developing an attitude of gratitude. It's important to share your wealth. Your wealth can be your talents, your time, or your treasures.

Inner work also includes getting comfortable with the idea of having more money than just what is needed to cover the basics of food, clothing, and shelter. You can't expect to earn or attract more money if you are not comfortable with the idea of having more money. It's also important to respect yourself.

Respecting yourself means making the right decisions with the money you currently have.

The outer work of achieving financial health means learning and practicing new money skills and behaviors:

- Ask for help learning about and managing your money if you need it.

- Get a financial advisor.

- Talk to someone you know who manages their money well.

- Balance your accounts.

- Know where your money goes.

- Identify where you're spending your money and be honest about it.

- Cut your expenses if you need to do so to get out of debt and start building wealth.

- Always try to pay your bills on time so you can eliminate debt.

- Start saving as early as possible. Most experts recommend saving at least 10 percent of your income. Once you have stable work, start saving 10 to 15 percent of each paycheck.

- Work on repairing your credit report and score. Most people know the importance of having good credit.

- Use a bookkeeping system if you need to. Do so by hand or go online and use QuickBooks or a similar program.

- Create a personal spending plan that you will honor.

When you invest in your present, you are investing in your future. When you invest in your future, you are investing in you. An excellent book that teaches how and where to start managing money is *Start Late and Finish Rich*, by David Bach. It's an easy read, with equally easy-to-apply strategies to help you plan a life of financial health and well-being.

That is the inner and outer work of how to achieve financial health. Simple strategies. Allow those strategies to compound over time. Take small steps when you're making changes, and those small steps will equal significant results over time, and a lot more money in your pocket!

PUTTING IT ALL TOGETHER—A ROAD MAP FOR YOUR HEALTH AND HAPPINESS

If you have an idea of where you are and where you want to go in your life, if you have a road map to follow, it will be easier to get there. If you were traveling from Chicago to Los

Angeles, you would eventually get to Los Angeles if you just headed west; hopefully, but it would be a lot easier and quicker if you had a road map. The same holds true for your health and happiness. If you can break down your goals and what you need to do to achieve them, you will be much more successful in achieving health and happiness.

Where to Start? Dealing With Being Overwhelmed

The information I've laid out may be great, or just okay for some of you, but it's not going to be very useful if you don't have a good starting point. When people consider making changes to their health and creating a sense of happiness and satisfaction, they are often not sure where to start.

First, list the areas of your life that need attention. Then, identify several things you can do to make positive changes in those respective areas, and break them down into small action steps. Start with the most comfortable action step. Incrementally and progressively, those small steps will lead you to your goal. The most successful way I have found to achieve any goal is to break it down and take it one step at a time.

To overcome feelings of being overwhelmed, identify and commit to the smallest steps first. When you take that first small step, you will likely achieve success, and when you take the second step, you will feel a sense of accomplishment. This will allow you to become a little more confident, so you look forward to taking the third step. When you take the third step, you will feel more momentum and a greater sense of accomplishment, which will inspire you to further action.

This series of steps compounds in its effectiveness. Rarely does our road map play out exactly as we created it, however. More often than not, there are detours or roadblocks. Inevitably, if you keep following your plan of action, you will achieve your goals of health and happiness.

Happiness Is an Inside Job

Believe it or not, happy people are happy because they make a decision to be satisfied. Often, it's a decision we make ahead of time to change the way we think. We can actually learn to create happiness on demand. There are several benefits of happiness. There are biological benefits, social benefits, mental and cognitive benefits, emotional benefits, and financial benefits.

Biologically, happy people tend to have lower blood pressure, lower cholesterol, and better sleep; they metabolize food and burn fat more easily and are typically more physically fit.

Who would you spend more time with—someone who is happy, or someone who is grouchy?

Exactly. Happy people tend to have better relationships. They have more friends. They get invited to more social events. They get asked out on more dates. They get more marriage proposals. Happy people have a better social life.

In terms of the mental and cognitive benefits of happiness, happy people learn more quickly. They can recall and integrate information more easily. They solve problems easier, and they tend to find solutions more readily. There are great and obvious cognitive benefits to learning and deciding to be happy.

Emotionally, making a decision to be happy simply feels better. I personally believe we are designed to be happy, but life is always better with at least one good friend, and although no one can quite agree on how many more muscles it takes to smile rather than frown, smiling burns more calories.[54] There are financial benefits, too. Happy people tend to be more productive and more efficient. They have better problem-solving skills, so they tend to get more raises, more promotions, and more job opportunities.

Being happy is all about perspective. You decide whether the glass is half full or half empty. To develop a habit of happiness, focus on being grateful; focus on solutions to problems rather than spending time and energy focusing on the problem. Always look for the lessons and gifts in your experiences.

Make peace with yourself and pay attention to your thoughts. Substitute positive thoughts for negative thoughts.

Nourish your body. Energize your body with exercise because that produces endorphins, and endorphins help you feel happy. Happy people practice the habit of forgiveness, and they make a point of spreading kindness. When you spread kindness, you make it contagious.

Happy people continually find ways to connect to something bigger than themselves. Try to find your passion. Be of service to others. "Lose the news" is something I always stress with my clients, and it is something I'm mindful of myself. The news is stressful and depressing, and it's often inaccurate.

One of the best ways to feel better about yourself and the world is to stop listening to popular media, whether it's via TV, radio, newspapers, magazines, or information you read on the internet.

Finally, learn to see the world as the kind place that it really is. Yes, bad things happen in our world, and to all of us, at one time or another. But how we choose to think about what happens determines how we will feel about it. No matter what is happening to us or around us, the one thing we can always choose is our attitude.

Living in Harmony: Examples of a Balanced Lifestyle

Living in harmony involves learning to create and have peace within yourself and toward others in the world. Part of living in harmony is about forgiveness.

I stress to my clients *the forgiveness set*, a set of three very powerful and effective affirmations:

- *I forgive myself.*

- *I forgive others.*

- *I am forgiven.*

Look for creating balance in your work life, in your play, in your rest. Create financial stability. To live a life of harmony, you will need to focus your attention on what really matters.

If living a more authentic life—one that reflects your values, visions, and ethics—appeals to you, you must commit to honoring and loving yourself. That means having good relationships. How can you establish or redefine your life and create healthy relationships if you are not looking to create peaceful, harmonious relationships?

How do you create a harmonious life?

First, identify what is getting in the way. There are typically seven roadblocks that get in the way of being able to create a harmonious life:

1. The first roadblock is a belief that taking care of yourself is not right.

2. The second roadblock points to your schedules and commitments. They may not reflect your priorities.

3. The third roadblock is that you feel drained by places, people, and things, such as daily tasks with work, children, or your household.

4. The fourth roadblock is feeling trapped by money. You are unable to make the choices you really want to make because of debt or other financial issues.

5. The fifth roadblock is stress. Maybe stress has become the primary source of fuel in your life. You are always running from one thing to the next without time to slow down and regroup.

6. The sixth roadblock is feeling isolated. You may be missing a supportive community in your life. All too often, we feel isolated, lonely, or disconnected. Most of us long to share a deeper connection with others.

7. The seventh roadblock is your spiritual well-being. It often takes the last place, if not being absent altogether. Maybe you'd like to spend more time doing things that

feed your soul such as yoga, meditation, reading, time in nature, or prayer. But life gets in the way.

If you are willing to make some changes, even small changes, and allow those to compound over time, your life will change dramatically. You should make improving the quality of your life your main focus.

Some strategies facilitate living a life of balance and harmony. Take good self-care. This means your work is not your life. Again, that means making sure you have healthy relationships. Your relationships shape you and add meaning to your life, so you want to make sure you are spending time with people who are supportive of you and are encouraging.

Another strategy for good self-care involves minding your emotional and physical health. Stress impacts both. Identify what feels right and incorporate more of that in your life.

Your spiritual well-being is part of self-care, as well as finding ways to have fun and be adventurous. Contribute to others. When your cup is full, you naturally want to share.

Another aspect of self-care is to be of service to others because being of service brings us closer in a way that adds richness to our lives.

Self-care involves connecting your head with your heart. Living in your head keeps you disconnected from how you feel. As Nicole Autenburg says, "A connection between your head and your heart is essential to living well. Without it, you will end up sleepwalking through life."[55]

Self-care includes learning to listen to your wise or higher self. Just like we talked about in feeding your soul, keep a positive attitude. Your attitude is the one thing that you can always control, no matter what the circumstances. Be assertive, not aggressive. Being assertive is expressing your thoughts and feelings directly in a way that is respectful and kind, but honest.

Another way to live a life in harmony is to get your priorities in order. Take control of what gets your time and attention and stop reacting to life. Start managing it. Set new priorities. Learn strategies to help ensure your priorities are honored. Believe it or not, you have a choice about how you live your life. You can continue as you are and remain stuck, or you can do something about it.

Three things to help get your priorities straight are:

1. Assess how you spend your time. This will tell you where your current priorities are. Define your new priorities based on what is essential for your whole life. Honor your new priorities by committing to spending more time on them. That means folding your priorities into

your everyday life. Say no to extra activities unless they are an absolute yes. Schedule time for life. Set healthy boundaries for yourself and others.

2. Identify and eliminate the energy drainers in your life: people, things, disorganized spaces.

3. Invest in your financial health.

Living a life of harmony can also be achieved by kicking adrenaline habits. High stress levels over time can lead to heart disease, diabetes, insomnia, chronic fatigue, and increased conflicts. All these undermine your ability to be at your best in your body, mind, spirit, and, indeed, your relationships. There are healthier ways to fuel your body and healthier ways to fuel your life.

A soulful community can also help you have a harmonious life. Build high-quality relationships that enhance your life instead of relationships that detract from your life. Build relationships that support, encourage, and challenge you to be your best.

Lastly, honor your spiritual well-being. Arguably the most crucial relationship is the connection to your higher self. At some point, most of us long for more meaning in our lives—a sense of purpose and a connection to something greater.

Living in harmony also involves allowing people to love you. Allow people to give to you and receive their love in all the ways that they want to give it.

Living in harmony involves developing the ability to understand yourself and to act in higher ways. Everything that happens to you in life should help you know yourself better and make you a better person. Look for the goodness in people, and, when you do, you will most certainly find it.

Believe in your success. Picture yourself as having what you want and living in integrity. This means living the truth. It means acting, talking, and behaving in ways that honor yourself and others.

You deserve to have a beautiful life filled with love, abundance, excellent health, good friends, and loving relationships. There is an increasing harmony that comes as you begin to balance and enjoy your life. Affirm your commitment to yourself by living a life of design and harmony.

To illustrate these points, I remember a personal experience with divorce. To say that experiencing divorce is one of the most devastating experiences that anybody can have throughout their life is probably an understatement.

My happiness, my harmony, and my financial health were all undermined during that time. Mostly, I had to learn to pick up the pieces. I am fortunate that I am in a position to understand how the mind works and the importance of action steps.

Being as overwhelmed as I was, I can't tell you how many days I was engulfed in feelings of despair—it became vitally important that I regroup. I had to find a way to forgive and recreate peace in my life. I had to find a way to create harmony, both in myself, and in my relationships. And I had to find a way to recover financially, as well.

I realized during some of those darkest nights that happiness is still something that I can create. No matter what was going on around me, happiness was, and always will be, a choice. It's about choosing to find the goodness in your life, choosing to find the abundance. And again, that also meant that I had to find and choose ways to create a new financial plan for myself.

That divorce left me with a different standard of living. That was when I made it a point to specifically learn about understanding my money mindset.

I learned that no matter our circumstances, if we learn to think about money differently, if we learn to create different action steps, we can put ourselves in a position to achieve financial health and even financial abundance.

That divorce experience allowed me to see that this was not only possible, but also predictable, if I identified the small steps needed and then committed to taking the needed action.

CHAPTER 5

ARE YOU YOUR GREATEST ASSET OR LIABILITY?

HOW MUCH IS YOUR HEALTH REALLY WORTH?

Believe it or not, you are either your greatest asset or your greatest liability. Whether you realize it or not, you are ultimately responsible for all your choices. Once you get to an age of knowing what's what, no matter what the influences are—media, word of mouth, friends, messages, and behavioral examples passed on through generations— ultimately, you are the one who is responsible for your health.

When I say *health*, I mean all aspects of health—body, mind, and spirit. When I say *body*, I mean your physical health and your financial health. When I say *mind*, I mean intellectually, logically, and emotionally. When I refer to your spiritual health, I mean the strength of your connection with something greater than yourself, and how much joy and peace you have in your life.

Your choices will determine whether or not you are working for your health or against your health. The sum of all your choices determines what kind of life you have. Everything compounds, which I will be speaking more about later, but all your decisions today influence the next choice and the next choice after that.

In this chapter, I help you decide whether you currently are your greatest asset or liability. If you are your most significant liability, how can you become your greatest asset?

The Cost of an Unhealthy Lifestyle—The Impact on You, Your Family, and Your Community

It's hard to put a dollar amount on the cost of your health, but experts agree that most people spend the highest amount of money in the last ten years of their lives. Typically, lots of the money is spent on prescriptions and medical care. When you start early to take care of your health, as soon as your knowledge or your awareness is heightened, you will save money. You will also have lower costs emotionally—the impact on your mood and mental health—and physically, as it relates to your physical health.

Remember, all the lifestyle diseases are preventable. The term *lifestyle diseases* includes all autoimmune disorders, heart disease, diabetes, most cancers, incidents of early-onset stroke, and most dementias, to name the most significant. All these are preventable, and many of them are treatable and even reversible. Your thoughts, feelings, and actions determine the impact on your lifestyle. You can be your best friend or your worst enemy.

Whatever is happening to you affects your family and your community.

Do you want to be a burden to your family because of your ill physical, emotional, and financial health? Or do you want to be an asset to your family?

How about your community? When you are unhealthy, everyone in your life is affected either directly or indirectly. For example, when I talk about community impact, I'm asking whether you can be a viable member of your community. That includes your work community.

If you are not at your best, then most likely, you won't be as effective or as productive as you could be or should be. Consequently, that means your work is going to suffer. What does that mean for your coworkers? What does that mean for your company and for your family? If you are struggling and are unhealthy, that has a direct impact on your ability to earn.

Most bankruptcies that are filed in this country are a result of medical expenses.[56]

Whether you realize it or not, the cost of an unhealthy lifestyle is exponential. You are solely responsible for creating a life of health, a life of happiness. No one can do that for you. As you will learn in the next section, that needs to be earned.

A Healthy Lifestyle Is Earned

If you want a healthy lifestyle—a life of vitality, strength, energy, financial health, and spiritual health—you will then you have to earn them. No one is going to give that to you. Believe it or not, and this may challenge some people; you are not entitled to a healthy lifestyle. While it may sound a little tough to believe, a healthy lifestyle must be earned. But the good news is, everything we need to earn that healthy lifestyle is given to us free at birth—our minds.

What do I mean by that? Most of us, if we are fortunate, are born into a healthy body. Once we get to the age when we can choose how active we are, what we eat, and how we live, we need to invest. That means we need to be disciplined. We need to invest time to get enough exercise and rest. We need to invest effort—to keep our bodies fit. We need to invest in our emotional and mental discipline because we are all creatures of habit. Forty to 90 percent of our day-to-day functioning is habit-based.[57] That means it's unconscious and automatic.

If you are currently living a lifestyle that you don't feel is in your best interest, or if you are your most significant liability, then you need to choose to earn your way to good health: physically, financially, and emotionally. This means taking time to educate yourself on what you can do to begin to create a healthy lifestyle. That may mean trading off certain activities in your life to make room for fitness. For example, that may mean less TV time in exchange for more time to exercise. That may mean less time with friends for more time to prepare food for the week ahead.

Ultimately, if you are going to live a life of health, wealth, and happiness, it must be earned. You are worth it.

Your Return on Investment (ROI)

Some of you may be familiar with the term Return on Investment, or ROI. It's a financial term that means whatever you put in as an investment is going to determine what you get back in return. Your ROI isn't only limited to financial investments. Your return will always be in direct proportion to what you choose to invest, in any area of your life. If you want to be happy, more productive, and more energized, if you wish to experience better moods and increased cognitive functioning; less debt and a more reasonable work lifestyle, then you must realize they all depend on how much effort you put into those areas of your life. Again, you cannot expect any kind of return if you are not making an investment.

This is why I say you are not entitled to a healthy lifestyle. You must invest in your lifestyle. Some people think that if they just think about it, visualize it, feel it emotionally, then it's going to happen, but that is backward thinking. It's almost like the story of the old man who is feverishly rubbing his hands in front of the wood-burning stove saying, "Give me heat" when he hasn't yet put wood in it. If you are not investing, then the return on your investment is going to be zero.

You need to set a reasonable plan, incremental and progressive in nature, and realize this is a long-term investment. It's a marathon; take it slow and steady. If you can continue to make those incremental changes and let them compound over time, then you will see that over the long term, you will have a much better quality of life. You will have healthier relationships and a body that you can be proud of, and you will get better sleep. You will be more productive at work, and you will have a life that you absolutely enjoy because you've earned that return on your investment.

I'd like you to realize that you must move from being dependent, or codependent, on the health insurance model and understand that it is broken. Our current health insurance model is designed to keep people sick, simply because it's focused on symptom management, and not on prevention and cure.

I encourage all of you reading this book to consider working with a physician who is not constrained by the services they can provide based on the insurance model. Instead, find a provider who has all the services you need. Be willing to invest in your health (even if you have to pay out of pocket for those services) and break free of depending on your health insurance to get you healthier. It's just not going to happen.

Those of you who continue to rely on the health insurance model are going to get sicker and sicker, and more and more disillusioned. You are responsible for your health. That means you must choose to pay for the services that you need and that you deserve, whether they are covered by insurance or not.

EXAMINING YOUR LIFESTYLE

You must examine your lifestyle, because you need to know where you are to create a road map of success. You should take a close, honest look at where you are now, what the issues are— physically, mentally, emotionally, financially—and decide what you need to do about them. If you are not examining your lifestyle, you probably will not reach your goals of health and wellness.

Getting Real With Yourself

Getting real with yourself means you must be honest. You need to examine your lifestyle. You need to consider the foods you're eating. You need to question how often, if at all, you're moving your body. You need to evaluate your sleep habits—both the quantity of sleep and the quality of it. You need to ask yourself whether you have a healthy work/life balance. You need to examine your relationships. All these aspects of your life affect your health and your happiness. You need to *get real*.

For me, that meant considering what I do on a day-to-day basis. I experienced a health crisis a couple years ago related to adrenal fatigue. As I said, I was working ungodly hours. I was eating a lot of fast food. Because I was working so much, I was not exercising nearly as much as I should have been. Of course, as a result, my sleep was affected. I was not getting nearly enough sleep. My lifestyle choices were now compounding in a negative direction. My health and my happiness were declining.

The first thing I had to do was sit down and ask myself: *Aimee, what's going on? You're tired. You're anxious. You're irritable.* I had to get honest with myself. I needed to make some changes to the foods I bought and what I ate. I needed to recreate a healthy lifestyle. I needed to reexamine my work schedule and make changes. I really needed to get real with myself.

If you are going to achieve the results you want in your life, you need to do the same. That means getting honest and stop making excuses. You can't blame other people for your choices. You are the one who must take ownership. Be encouraged. Put yourself in a position of power and mastery, not just over your health, but over everything in your life. One of the best things you can do is learn to take ownership of your choices. Get real with yourself.

The Compounding Effects

When I talk about the *compounding effects*, which is a common term used in the financial industry, I mean everything adds up. Everything will either add up to your betterment or to your detriment; your thoughts, actions, and choices all build upon themselves.

When making changes in your lifestyle—lasting and sustainable changes—you have to start small. But with compounding effects, even small changes can yield significant results. We can see this with compounding interest. It's laid out beautifully in our academic learning model. We start off with addition and subtraction, and then we move on to multiplication and division, and so on. If we started at the division, we would get lost completely. We start with small changes and let all those small changes build upon themselves. The thing about small changes is that they are not going to be overwhelming.

When I first started making changes in my lifestyle, I just simply added more good foods, for example, more vegetables. Since I had not been working out at all, I scheduled one to two workouts a week. If I could do more, that was a bonus.

Making small changes allows our emotional mind not to be overwhelmed. One of the biggest mistakes people make is taking on too much at one time. When that happens, we may have a burst of motivation and enthusiasm, but usually, within two weeks, we are overwhelmed, because our logical and emotional mind cannot keep up with the amount of focus and time needed to tackle those significant changes. The best way to sustain change is to identify small steps. Make them incremental and progressive. Progressive means you build on those steps bit by bit.

Advocating for Your Health

Probably one of the most important pieces of advice I can impart is to ask questions. Ask questions of the people who are giving you information. Ask questions of your healthcare providers. It has been my clinical experience that patients and clients who get the best outcomes are the ones who advocate for their health. That means they are asking lots of questions.

We are taught that doctors know everything, but they don't. They certainly know a lot, and they are credible experts. But the reality is we only know as much as we have learned. What most healthcare providers have learned, if you are following the conventional medical model, is the curriculum that is designed and implemented by big pharmaceutical companies.

When you are meeting with your healthcare provider, and they are making a recommendation, ask questions. Older generations, all too often, don't ask questions because they were taught that doctors are the ultimate authority. They simply follow directions, but their health has suffered as a consequence.

Many of us in our middle- to late-adulthoods need to care for our elderly parents who are sick. Many elders are still reluctant to ask questions, despite the support of a child who may be accompanying them to their doctor visit.

But you need to learn to advocate for your health because no one can do it for you. That means taking the time to learn on your own. We have a wealth of resources online. While not everything you read online is right or can be trusted, if you take your time and do enough research, you will start to find some common themes. Trust me; if there are problems, there are always solutions to those problems.

Decide that you are going to be your greatest asset and start advocating for your health. Ask questions, research, take responsibility for your health. Be open to learning. Be a sponge and absorb everything you can. Think critically, knowing that ultimately you have to find your truth if you're going to be successful in all these areas of life. You, your family, your loved ones, your community, and even your employer will be most appreciative that you are advocating for your health.

If you happen to be at a healthcare provider's office, I highly recommend you bring someone with you. Often, when we are stressed or anxious and don't understand what is going on with our health, we can mishear or misunderstand, or miss altogether, what is being said. Two sets of eyes, two sets of ears, two sets of questions. List your questions ahead of time and bring the list with you, so you can be sure to ask them.

You will often feel rushed, so make sure to say, "Hold on, I have some questions that still need to be asked and answered." If your doctor continues to rush you or refuses to educate you, consider finding another provider. You're entitled to be educated about your health, especially since you're paying for that office visit!

Take notes because, during your conversation, there may be some points you don't understand, and you will want to ask about them at that appointment or at your next follow-up appointment. Always try to bring someone with you whenever you are meeting with a healthcare provider. Knowing the truth will set you free.

A RECIPE FOR SUCCESS

Much like a food recipe, if you follow the directions, you are likely to get the desired results. A step-by-step approach breaks things down for us and makes it easier for us to follow. We don't have to guess.

If you want a recipe for your health success, I recommend you start by working with a health coach, an expert, someone who has the education, training, knowledge, and expertise that can help create the recipe for your success. What is right for one body may not be right for every body, as I have said before.

If you follow the recipe, whether it's the one that is on the back of your shampoo bottle that says "Wash, rinse, and repeat" or the saying "Eat, sleep, and move," you are likely to get good results. In this section, I would like to introduce you to how you can create a recipe for your own success.

Emotional Mind Versus Logical Mind

To be successful you need to understand that your mind works in different ways. You have an emotional mind, which is your prehistoric, reptilian mind. You have a logical mind, which is your prefrontal cortex, your reasoning mind. They don't always work hand in hand.

To be successful, you need to understand how those two minds work. Often, they work against each other. Nine out of ten times, when the emotional mind is in conflict with the logical mind, the emotional mind will win out. Speaking from the standpoint of evolution, your emotional mind is the oldest part of your brain-mind. It's millions of years old, and your prefrontal cortex, your logical mind, is only thousands of years old.

To create lasting change, you need to work with the emotional mind. You can use your logical mind to create a recipe for success, the *how-to*, but for change to be sustained, you need to reinforce all your little incremental steps because the emotional mind typically likes things to stay the same. Prehistorically, sameness equaled predictability, and predictability equaled safety. Your emotional mind prefers things to remain the same. That means it prefers to do things habitually.

Habitually means unconsciously, automatically; and, surprisingly, habits require very little caloric energy. In prehistoric times, the best thing we could do to conserve energy was to create habits. That meant doing the same things over, and over again. If we are going to change and create a healthy lifestyle, we cannot continue to do things the same as we have. But we must work within the constraints of the emotional mind.

For changes to be lasting, the emotional mind needs to feel like the effort is and was worth it. This means you have to reward yourself along the way.

If you are exercising once a week, you'd better celebrate that once-a-week exercise episode! If you are going to bed early to get more sleep, you'd better praise yourself for making an effort, because the only way those changes are going to be sustained from an emotional standpoint that keeps you motivated and excited is to find some way to convince yourself that the difference is worth it.

Any physical changes you pursue are not going to happen right away. You should reward yourself for the work as you move forward. That means finding ways to positively reinforce your efforts.

I usually praise myself, or literally pat myself on the back, for a job well done. I recommend that you find a way to reinforce your emotional mind for the steady efforts it's making along your journey to health and happiness.

How Habits Are Formed

Habits are formed one action and one thought at a time. I know this sounds ridiculously elementary, but it's true. They build one at a time, then they compound. Everything that you do over and over again ultimately forms a habit, but only if you do it long enough.

It's helpful to think that you can form a new habit in eighteen to twenty-one days. That is absolutely not true. You can set a minimal neural pathway in place, but for something to become a real, lasting habit, it's going to take at least 90 to 180 days.

Habits are formed by following a set of actions or thoughts—whether it's a thought habit, a behavioral habit, or a spiritual habit—one action at a time, and letting those actions compound through repetition. And you always need to positively reinforce those new action steps. They are not habits yet, and they require extra attention, as well as mental and physical effort.

If they are not nurtured, if they are not watered like you would water a new garden, they are never going to create a robust neural pathway, and that is really what is needed for new behaviors or thought patterns to take hold and become automatic, unconscious habits. When you engage in an action over and over again, that strengthens the neural pathways, which, in turn, creates more and more of them.

I often joke that I started to play the saxophone because I like to toot my own horn, but that's not true. It's because I love jazz music. I learned to play the saxophone to create a greater sense of joy and fulfillment, a greater sense of spiritual connection in my life. However, if I ever hoped to get better at playing the saxophone, I knew that I had to commit to that same action over and over again. When I was learning, I had to remember to practice.

That is not necessarily exciting, depending on what the action is, but that is how habits are formed: consistently engaging in the same type of thinking, or actions, repeatedly until you have created a robust set of neural pathways, and it becomes unconscious and automatic.

Celebrate Your Success

As I said before, for change to be successful and lasting, you must find a way to positively reinforce yourself. You must celebrate your success. You should reward small efforts repeatedly.

Your long-term success is aided by spending time with like-minded people. These are people who are either en route to achieving their healthy lifestyle goals or have already achieved them. They could be a coach, people in a support group, in a group of physical or personal training or those at a spiritual center, at a drumming circle, or even at a yoga studio.

This applies to celebrating success as well. You can help support and encourage the success of others while they help foster your success. If you don't celebrate your successes, you will likely not continue to take the action steps that allow you to have a healthy lifestyle with a healthy body, mind, and spirit. Since good health is not a given, and you have earned it, you deserve to celebrate your success. Savor it.

When you have achieved one goal, take time to really enjoy that, and then set the next goal. Enjoy the journey along the way. When you have achieved your next goal, savor that as well. Always celebrate your success. It gets your mind, your body, and your spirit into a habit of leading a successful lifestyle.

The way to lead a successful lifestyle is to make one right choice after another as best as you can and let those choices compound. Then celebrate along the way.

Follow the recipe, master it, and allow for modifications as you go. Your health goals may change, depending on your stage of life. But always follow the recipe.

Conclusion

Thank you for taking the time to read my book. I want to leave you with a sense of hope, inspiration, and the *how-to* of living a life of health and happiness in all areas. If you found any part of this book helpful, please bless others by sharing what you've learned.

It's been said that every person accidentally influences 10,000 people in their lifetime. Imagine the positive impact you can have on so many more people when you are living your life with purpose and direction and living a healthy, happy life—a life of fulfillment.

Imagine being a role model for everyone in your life.

What is the worth of your new knowledge to you and your loved ones? I want you to be able to write your own *prescription* for healthy living. Making any change in any area of your life will undoubtedly affect every other aspect of your life. Your body, mind, and spirit are simply aspects of your wholeness.

While it is easier to talk about these areas as separate entities, the truth is you are one integrated whole. This means that change in one area of your life affects change in you as a whole. And when you start to see, feel, or realize positive changes in your life, those changes will begin to create an increased sense of confidence and momentum, which will beautifully position you to continue making more positive changes.

Everything begins with a decision. You must decide that living a better life is important enough for you to take action. Reading this book is taking action. Decide if you want to continue taking additional action for even more excellent benefits.

Again, I recommend starting by evaluating what area or aspect—body, mind, or spirit—is most readily amenable to making small, positive changes. Maybe it's finding a new healthcare provider or coach that understands and practices a truly integrative approach. Perhaps it's committing to learning and practicing deep breathing for two minutes a day. Maybe it's taking time out every morning or evening to count your blessings.

No matter where you start, start small and let your actions and results compound. If you try to change too many things at once, you will most likely be overwhelmed and quit. Start small, stay the course, and celebrate your successes along the way.

Finally, I would like to invite you to stay connected with my team of change agents and me. You can read our integrative health and wellness blog posts on a variety of topics relevant to everyday living. Additionally, we host online and live presentations that you may be interested in attending.

You can enjoy and continue to learn how to create health, wealth, and happiness through our ever-expanding podcasts. You can also listen to my weekly radio show, *Mind Over Matters* on AM 820 every Sunday morning at 10:00 a.m. CST. You can also listen to a rebroadcast on Soundcloud.com or visit our website at TheCIFHW.com or visit our Facebook page at Facebook.com/thecifhw.

Wherever or whenever you join us, we welcome the opportunity to grow together with you. I wish you much success, happiness, and health.

With love,

Dr. Aimee

Next Steps

Congratulations! Now that you've read my book, I'd like to invite you to continue to take the next step in creating your life by design.

To help you create more health, wealth, and happiness in your life, please check out our website: TheCIFHW.com. Check in to receive special promotional offers and updates on our training and events.

My team and I welcome the opportunity to work side by side with you as partners in determining your best direction for creating positive, lasting change in your life. To get started, you can call us at 630.980.1400 or visit us online at theCIFHW. com or facebook.com/thecifhw. Be well.

Endnotes

1 Benatar, S. R. "Global disparities in health and human rights: A critical commentary." *Am J Public Health.* 1998.

2 Selgelid, M. J. "Ethics and Infectious Disease." Bioethics. 2005. doi:10.1111/j.1467–8519.2005.00441.x

3 World Bank. World Development Indicators. datatopics. worldbank.org/world-development-indicators/

4 Goldman, Dana and Darius Lakdawalla. "The Global Burden of Medical Innovation." Brookings Institution. Jan 30, 2018. brookings.edu/research/the-global-burden-of-medical-innovation/

5 Hogg, Peter. "The Top Medical Advances in History." Proclinical. proclinical.com/blogs/2021-6/the-top-10-medical-advances-in-history

6 United Nations. World Economic Situation and Prospects 2019. un.org/development/desa/dpad/wp-content/uploads/sites/45/WESP2019_BOOK-web.pdf

7 eytonsearth.org/brown-recluse-bite-clay.html; mindbodygreen.com/articles/bentonite-clay-benefits-uses-safety-precautions-and-more; earthsclaystore.com/

products/calcium-bentonite-clay-powder; nykaa.com/
aztec-secret-food-grade-calcium-bentonite-powder-for-
detoifying-in-and-out-for-men-women/p/834162; webmd.
com/a-to-z-guides/bentonite-clay-benefits; medicalnewstoday.
com/articles/325241#removing-toxins-from-the-body;
commonsensehome.com/home-remedies-for-bug-bites-and-
stings/

8 Mercier, B., J. Prost, and M. Prost. "The Essential Oil of
Turpentine and Its Major Volatile Fraction (Alpha- and Beta-
Pinenes): A Review." *Int J Occup Med Environ Health.* 2009.
22(4):331–342. doi:10.2478/v10001-009-0032-5

9 karger.com/Article/Fulltext/381546; medicinenet.com/
immunizations/article.htm

10 med.unc.edu/phyrehab/pim/wp-content/uploads/
sites/615/2018/03/Evidence-Based-Med.pdf

11 hopkinsmedicine.org/news/media/releases/
study_suggests_medical_errors_now_third_leading_cause_
of_death_in_the_us

12 mstbrazil.org/news/scientist-argues-
%E2%80%9Cglyphosate%E2%80%9D-will-lead-autism-50-
children-2025

13 census.gov/popclock/

14 commonwealthfund.org/publications/issue-briefs/2020/jan/us-health-care-global-perspective-2019; healthsystemtracker.org/chart-collection/infant-mortality-u-s-compare-countries/#item-infant-mortality-is-higher-in-the-u-s-than-in-comparable-countries_2019

15 fiercepharma.com/special-report/top-10-ad-spenders-big-pharma-for-2020

16 voicesforaffordablehealth.com/your-cost-watch/textbook-authors-big-pharma-industry/; globalnews.ca/news/5738386/canadian-medical-school-funding/

17 Kirsch, Irving and David Antonuccio. PDAP. "Antidepressants Versus Placebos: Meaningful Advantages Are Lacking." *Psychiatric Times*. Vol 19 No 9. 2002. psychiatrictimes.com/view/antidepressants-versus-placebos-meaningful-advantages-are-lacking

18 desispeaks.com/evidence-based-medicine/

19 Walsh, William. *Nutrient Power: Heal Your Biochemistry and Heal Your Brain*. Skyhorse Publishing, 2014.

20 Walker, Matthew. *Why We Sleep*. Scribner, 2017.

21 advisory.com/en/daily-briefing/2019/05/02/health-care-costs

22 "How Much of Americans' paychecks go to health care, charted." 2019. advisory.com/en/daily-briefing/2019/05/02/health-care-costs

23 World Health Organization. "The Preamble to the Constitution of the World Health Organization as Adopted by the International Health Conference." Official Records of the World Health Organization. October 2006. who.int/governance/eb/who_constitution_en.pdf

24 aihm.org/vision/

25 nccih.nih.gov/about

26 ACIM. Definition of Integrative Medicine and Health. Introduction. Published 2018. Accessed August 10, 2019. imconsortium.org/about/introduction/

27 "Alternative Medicine." *Wikipedia.* en.wikipedia.org/wiki/Alternative_medicine

28 irishtimes.com/news/health/why-are-doctors-so-against-alternative-medicine-1.188177

29 iarp.org/how-does-reiki-work/

30 ncbi.nlm.nih.gov/pmc/articles/PMC5126026/

31 ncbi.nlm.nih.gov/pmc/articles/PMC5171223/

32 ncbi.nlm.nih.gov/pmc/articles/PMC5126026/

33 simplypsychology.org/maslow.html

34 ohsu.edu/womens-health/benefits-healthy-sex-life

35 cdc.gov/coronavirus/2019-ncov/need-extra-precautions/
people-with-medical-conditions.html

36 drdrewjohnson.com.ismmedia.com/ISM3/std-content/
repos/Top/Detoxification.pdf

37 Booth, F. W., C. K. Roberts, and M. J. Laye. "Lack of
exercise is a major cause of chronic diseases." *Compr Physiol.*
2012. doi:10.1002/cphy.c110025

38 Neufer, P. D., et al. "Understanding the Cellular and
Molecular Mechanisms of the Physical Activity-Induced
Health Benefits." *Cell Metab.* 2015. doi: 10.1016/j.
cmet.2015.05.011

39 livescience.com/59011-gluten-avoidance-different-
countries.htm

40 consumerlab.com

41 Pacific College of Oriental Medicine. "What is Alternative
Medicine?" Published 2018. Accessed August 11, 2019.
pacificcollege.edu/news/blog/2018/02/26/what-is-alternative-
medicine

42 chatelaine.com/health/is-alternative-medicine-effective/

43 aiin.healthcare/topics/business-intelligence/only-18-clinical-recommendations-are-evidence-based

44 sciencemediacentre.co.nz/coveringscience/types-of-scientific-evidence/

45 ncbi.nlm.nih.gov/pmc/articles/PMC1118259/

46 everydayhealth.com/alternative-health/the-basics.aspx

47 leadingedgehealth.org/2013/02/04/death-bed-cancer-to-cancer-free-in-60-days/

48 Jensen, B. *Come Alive.* 1st ed. Bernard Jensen Intl., 1997.

49 cdc.gov/nchs/pressroom/04news/adultsmedicine.htm

50 rosewellness.com/autoimmune-disease-treatment/; rosewellness.com/are-you-acidic-or-alkaline/

51 thehealthy.com/alternative-medicine/change-in-you-15-minutes-meditation/

52 al.com/business/2018/07/the_1_reason_for_divorce.html

53 marketwatch.com/story/older-people-fear-this-more-than-death-2016-07-18

54 nbcnews.com/better/health/good-company-why-we-need-other-people-be-happy-ncna836106; nzherald.co.nz/bay-of-plenty-times/news/fitness-zone-start-smiling-it-burns-the-calories/56MPACF6TRYRCO6JFGJZQJNFBQ/

55 nicolerautenberg.com/2016/07/28/connect-your-head-with-your-heart/

56 cnbc.com/2019/02/11/this-is-the-real-reason-most-americans-file-for-bankruptcy.html

57 helpingyouengineeryourfuture.com/habits-work-smarter.htm

About The Author

Dr. Aimee Harris-Newon is a double board-certified integrative and interventional psychologist, entrepreneur, international bestselling author, presenter, and master success coach. She is also a frequent speaker at Harvard University and has a postgraduate specialization in functional health and wellness. She is considered one of America's leading experts in integrative health and wellness and believes in a holistic approach to life—treating the mind, body, and spirit.

She is the director of The Center for Integrative and Functional Health and Wellness in Bloomingdale, Illinois serving clients and patients locally, nationally, and internationally.

What makes her truly unique and exceptional are her broad and deep skill sets and her approach to health and wellness. As the founder and director of Dr. Aimee and Associates, and The Center for Integrative and Functional Health and Wellness, Dr. Harris-Newon and her team of experts don't just treat symptoms; they solve health and life problems, create better outcomes, and change lives.

With more than twenty-five years of practice as an integrative healthcare provider and master success coach, Dr. Harris-Newon has built several successful businesses and has amassed over 60,000 direct hours working with individuals, families, government agencies, and companies, including FedEx, UPS, McDonald's, Red Bull, and the U.S Army. Dr. Harris-Newon has also been featured as a frequent guest on ABC, CBS, NBC, and FOX News.

She is the host of the *Mind Over Matters* weekly radio show on AM 820.

Made in the USA
Monee, IL
11 January 2023

25113149R00105